I0462695

Table of Contents

The Panasonic S1/S1R Menu System Simplified

by David Thorpe

Published in the United Kingdom

First Publishing Date July 2019

Introduction

The Panasonic S1 and S1R (I'll refer to them both as S1 from here on) are the company's first venture into the 36x24mm sensor Full Frame format, up to now dominated by the big two DSLR makers, Nikon and Canon and to a lesser extent by Sony. Panasonic has vast experience in the field of mirrorless cameras by virtue of its very successful Micro Four Thirds range. The S1 is closely based on the company's G9 Micro Four Thirds camera and shares with it many advanced advanced features. It also adds many features of its own, among them a new menu system, visual display of the stabilization system in action and the best EVF on any camera. Once you've tried this one, you won't want to go back to an optical finder! But no amount of technical wizardry makes you love a camera. What will make you love the camera is the sheer image quality from the big sensor and the physical size of the body, which facilitates superb handling and accessibility to the multitude of buttons and levers that control it. It has a hefty, weather sealed magnesium frame which make it feel every bit the professional level camera it is.

There's a lot to know about the Panasonic S1. LVF Display Speed? AF-Point Scope Setting? ELEC.? MECH.? Some settings are crucial, some just good to know. This book doesn't try to teach you photography, you wouldn't buy a camera like the S1 if you didn't know what you were doing! Its aim is to familiarise you with the menu and settings of the S1, what they do and why you might want to use them. It is true that the camera is a tool but like knowing your scales on a violin, mastery of the S1 will aid your aim of taking better pictures.

The menu system and controls of the S1 are well presented and logically laid out but with 6 sections containing around 180 main menu items, many of those with sub menus, even the most experienced user will sometimes find themselves scratching their head and wondering what an entry means. This small book goes through every menu choice and control and explains (a) what it does and (b) why you might want to do it. It may not inspire you in a literary sense but with its help you may find an S1 tailored to your personal taste inspiring to use. I sometimes give my opinion on the best setting. It is only my opinion from my personal experience. It is best treated it as merely a starting point for building your own experience.

At the end of the book I go though the menu items as I set them. The aim of this is to give you a working setup without having to learn what each item does straight away. As you use the camera with my settings you will find yourself thinking, "that's really annoying. If only I could change that." You most likely can. Find the item in question and change it. You now have an S1 a little more tailored to you than before. The aim, eventually, is to have a photographic tool that is personal to your needs. Actually, using the Custom settings and the ability to save and restore 10 favourite settings from an SD card gives 10 different S1s in one. If your interest is photographing the dim interiors of medieval churches using a tripod you might set your S1 to Aperture priority f8/ ISO 200/ AFS. You might also like to photograph your son playing football with his school team using Shutter Priority 1/1000th/ ISO

3200/ AFC. Your stand camera and your action camera are but a click apart on the Mode Dial. A further click could take you to your favourite video setting. It is that flexibility and the sheer image quality of the S1 that makes it so exciting. The sheer configurability and operational versatility of the S1 can make it seem more the province of the rocket scientist than the artist. Time spent learning what the Panasonic S1 can do and how to do it will be rewarded by better results and ever widening photographic horizons.

If you find any errors or have comments to make, please email me at books@dthorpe.net

S1 and S1R - the Differences

 The S1 and S1R are essentially the same camera, in that the the the body, controls and menus are all the same. The big differences are the price and the MegaPixel count. Neither of those make any material difference to this book but here is a list of differences between the cameras which should be borne in mind in the appropriate sections.

• S1 sensor 6000x4000px (24M) / S1R sensor 8368x5584 (46M)

• S1 High Resolution Mode 12000x8000 (96M) / S1R 16736x11168 (187M)

• S1 ISO 50-204800 / 50-51200 (with extended ranges set)

• 4K 50 or 60p video limit 30 minutes, all others unlimited / S1R 4K 50 or 60p 15 minutes, 4K 25 or 30p 30 minutes, FHD unlimited

• Burst mode max frames, 90 frames RAW unlimited JPG / S1R 40 RAW 50 JPG

• Battery life S1 400 frames / S1R 380 (this is pretty theoretical

1

Figures 1-35

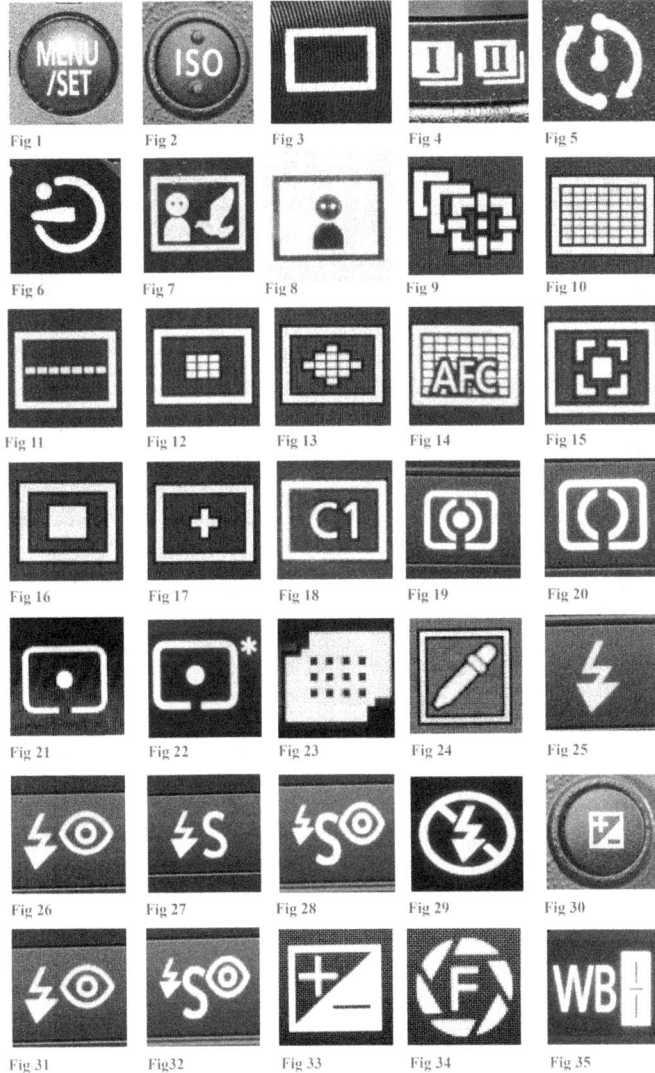

Fig 1 Fig 2 Fig 3 Fig 4 Fig 5

Fig 6 Fig 7 Fig 8 Fig 9 Fig 10

Fig 11 Fig 12 Fig 13 Fig 14 Fig 15

Fig 16 Fig 17 Fig 18 Fig 19 Fig 20

Fig 21 Fig 22 Fig 23 Fig 24 Fig 25

Fig 26 Fig 27 Fig 28 Fig 29 Fig 30

Fig 31 Fig32 Fig 33 Fig 34 Fig 35

Figures 36-63

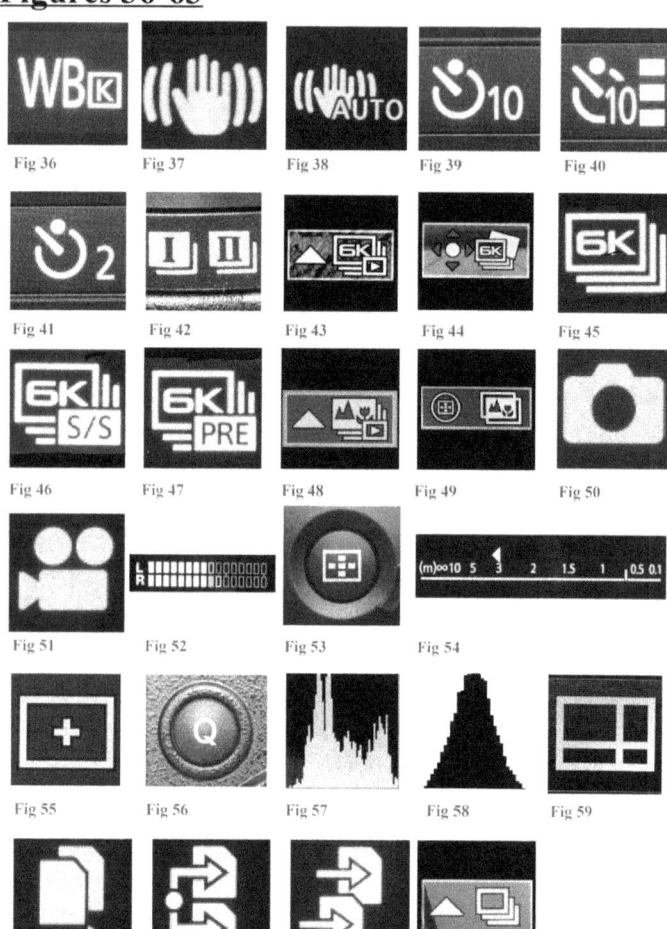

Fig 36

Fig 37

Fig 38

Fig 39

Fig 40

Fig 41

Fig 42

Fig 43

Fig 44

Fig 45

Fig 46

Fig 47

Fig 48

Fig 49

Fig 50

Fig 51

Fig 52

Fig 53

Fig 54

Fig 55

Fig 56

Fig 57

Fig 58

Fig 59

Fig 60

Fig 61

Fig 62

Fig 63

The Controls

The majority of control over a complex, dedicated imaging computer, which is what the S1 really is, is via the **Menu/Set button (Fig 01)**. There are a few things so basic that they must be controlled by exterior levers and buttons. Those controls do not differ greatly from the ones which film camera users from the previous century would have been familiar. Set the camera to M on the mode dial and you can control shutter speed and aperture directly. Press the **ISO button (Fig 02)** and you have changed the 'film' speed. The rest of the external controls are essentially shortcuts to often used menu items. Here is a brief rundown on the basics of the body controls of the S1. Refer to the key numbers below for an explanation of their function.

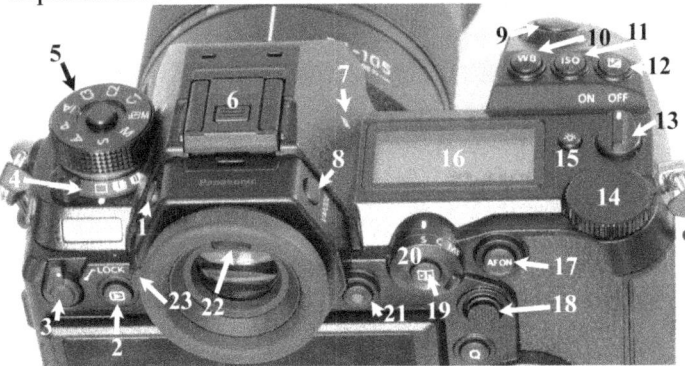

• 1 **LVF** (live View Finder) cycles between 3 selections, monitor on, eye level off/ monitor off, eye level on/ and auto switching between them. The obvious setting is auto but under some circumstances, when using a tripod and viewing on the monitor for example, your arm passing near the LVF sensor can cause it to switch to the eye level finder. If you are using the eye level finder and you take the camera from your eye to view the scene, the sensor will auto switch to the monitor. When you put the camera to your eye again, you must wait a moment for the auto switch to take place. In that time, the bird may have flown! Switching explicitly to the eye level finder prevents that. In **Setup→Monitor/Display 1→Eye Sensor** you have a a choice of **High** or **Low** sensitivity. **High** can be quite twitchy so **Low** is the general choice. Note that you can choose between monitor/ eye level/ auto in the **Eye Sensor** menu item too. If you find that convenient, you can free up the **LVF** button which can then be reassigned

• 2 The **Playback** button. After you have taken a picture, press this to review the image. You can, if you wish, review the image automatically by using the menu item **Auto Review** in the **Custom** menu.

• 3 The **Operation lock lever**. When turned to the right, the lock position, it disables any or all of the **Cursor** buttons,**Joystick**, **Touch screen**, **Front Dial**, **Rear Dial**, **Control Dial** and **Disp.** button. It comes into its own for item(s) that you wish to temporarily disable. For example, many photographers find that when using their S1 at eye level, the palm of their hand can brush against the **Cursor Dial** or the **Touch screen**, moving the focus area or altering a crucial setting at what might be a critical moment. Set these to the **Lock Lever** and you can toggle them on and off in a moment.

• 4 The **Drive Mode** dial. This sets the action of the shutter, whether it fires a single shot or a burst of shots for example. Set the dial in the position for normal single shot shooting **(Fig 03)** and the shutter will fire once every time you press the shutter button. However, what if you want to fire off a burst of frames or use the self-timer? Using the **Menus** you can set the **Self Timer** to, say, 2 seconds and **Burst Rate 1** to Medium, **Burst Rate 2** to **6K/4K**. The **Drive Mode** is how you tell your S1 to put them into action. Set to Burst Shot 1 or 2 **(Fig 04)** and the camera will shoot continuously at the speed you have set for them in **Photo→Others→Burst Shot 1/ Burst Shot 2 Setting**. Set to **Self Timer (Fig 06)** it will delay the shot for the time you have preset in the menu. Set to **Time Lapse/Stop Motion (Fig 05)** it will use whatever **Time Lapse** or **Animation** settings you have made. So, if you want the camera to make a time lapse sequence, have set all the parameters you want and it doesn't do it - it's because you haven't told it to with the **Drive Mode** dial.

• 5 The **Mode Dial**. This is the arguably most important control on the camera. The simplest setting is **iA**, Intelligent Auto. Set to this, the S1 becomes a point and shoot. You have limited control over how it takes the picture which makes it particularly irritating to experienced photographers like me because it is so often right! Your access to many menu items is greyed out in **iA** and the **AF Mode** button is disabled. **P** is for Program where the camera chooses the shutter speed and aperture. **A** is for Aperture Priority. You set the aperture, the camera varies the shutter speed to suit your setting. Aperture is the deciding factor in how much depth of field you have in your picture. For a portrait, you would probably want any distracting background elements to be blurred, in order to focus attention on your subject. For that you would limit your depth of field (obtain shallow depth of field) by using a wide aperture, that is opening your lens to its maximum f/3.5 or f/2.8, f/2 or f/1.4 if you have it. by Stop down to f/8 or lower and you have a wide depth of field so that you can get more of your picture in focus. If you are photographing a field of flowers, you can get flowers from near to far in focus. The downside to a small aperture is that to maintain the correct exposure, the shutter speed must be lower. This can lead to blurring of the image due to the camera moving during the exposure. Or, if there is anything moving in your picture, motion blurring. Which brings us to **S**, Shutter Priority. If you are photographing your children running around, they can move a surprisingly long way in, say 1/60th of a second. With **S** you can set a shutter speed fast enough to stop the motion blurring that a slow shutter speed would entail. The downside of a high shutter speed is that the lens aperture must be wider to bring in enough light for correct exposure. That, as I previously said, cuts your depth of field, making your focusing very critical, just what you don't want for a child's unpredictable movement. What the shutter speed gives, the aperture takes away and vice-versa. As with politics, exposure is the art of compromise. **M** Manual leaves you to set both shutter speed and aperture. It can't achieve anything that **A** or **S** don't but some people prefer to 'do it all'. **Note:** in all the previous, I have not mentioned the effect of the **ISO** setting. If you up the **ISO** setting you can have greater depth of field combined with higher shutter speeds. It looks like a win/win situation. Unfortunately, as with everyday life, there are very few win/win scenarios. As you raise the **ISO** setting, you are not increasing the amount of light , you are merely amplifying what you have. And as with a radio with a poor signal, the more you turn it up, the more background noise there is. On an imaging sensor, it manifests itself as a random 'rash' on your picture. This juggling act between shutter speed, aperture and ISO is at the heart of photography - only you can decide where your compromise will be. A handy use of **M** is to set the shutter speed and aperture you want and then set the **ISO** to **Auto**. That means you can set the shutter speed to stop movement and the aperture to provide adequate depth of field. They will not change because the S1 will vary the **ISO** to keep the exposure correct. It can't brighten the ambient light, though, so ultimately, handy or not, it is one more compromise. The other settings on the **Mode Dial** are less specific. **Creative Video** gives you full control over your **Movie** settings, in contrast to the **Rec** button (21) which when pressed starts your video using the settings you have set as your default in the **Movie** menu. While there are only 3 **C** positions on the dial, **C3** can actually store 10 sets of settings on its own, C3-1 through C3-10 and chosen by pressing the **Menu/ Set** button on the back of the camera after engaging **C3**.

• 6 The **Flash** hot shoe. Remove the sliding cover and slide the flash into the hotshoe there. On the front of the S1 below the **Drive Mode** dial , there is another flash contact with a screw in plug. That is the flash synch socket and is used to trigger studio lighting or other external flash. It only triggers the flash and has no electronic connection to it so cannot operate any auto flash functions. Most photographers nowadays will trigger external flashes automatically via the hot shoe.

• 7 The **Sensor Plane** mark. This is more useful for movie makers than stills. Movie makers usually shoot with manual focus to prevent unpleasant focus hunting. The Sensor Plane Mark provides an absolute point from which to measure the distance from a subject for setting focus distance on a lens. Although photographers often assume that distances are measured from the front of the lens, this can't be so since the front glass position changes according to zoom setting or the length of the lens.

• 8 The **V.Mode** button. This allows you to set the EVF image size. The maximum size is superb but for spectacle wearers might make the corners difficult to see and a bit blurred. There are 3 sizes available to choose from. However, this can work in conjunction with **Custom→Monitor/Display→LVF/Monitor Disp. Set** which allows you to view shooting information either superimposed on the image or on strips above and underneath it. I prefer an uncluttered image area with the biggest display possible so set the **EVF** to its maximum size with the information displayed outside the image area. It is this kind of tailoring that makes the S1 such a joy to use.

• 9 The **Shutter Release** button. No need to emphasize the importance of this. **Note:** it can be customized in **Custom→Focus/Shutter 2** by setting it to release the shutter and/or focusing with a half press. Incidentally, most camera mechanical shutters - **MECH.** on the S1 - have a rated life of 200,000 shots. The S1's is rated at twice that, 400,000. The **ELEC.** shutter, being entirely electronic, has unlimited life.

• 10 The **White Balance** button. If you look at an object in daylight and then indoors by artificial light, the object will appear the same colour in both environments. Although the daylight contains much blue light and the artificial light much red, your brain instinctively compensates for the environmental differences. The camera cannot do this and must be told the colour temperature (more blue=colder, more red=warmer). You can set **WB** explicitly for sunlight, cloudy, indoors and so on but in practise **Auto** is generally best. You can correct to some extent in post processing. **WB** is irrelevant when you are shooting **RAW** since it retains all the information from the image and can be set as you prefer afterwards. In the case of **RAW**, just set it to **Auto**. **Note:** Auto has 3 flavours. **AWB** is standard Panasonic colours. **AWBc** reduces the reddish hue under incandescent light sources, giving a more natural balance though there is also **AWBw** which retains the reddish hue. Many photographers prefer this last one for the warm atmosphere it imparts to indoor picture. This becomes less and less important as **LED** lighting, which usually has a daylightish colour balance, becomes established in the home.

• 11 The **ISO** button. **ISO** is the sensitivity of your camera's sensor to light. If the exposure at the light level in an indoor sports stadium yields an exposure of 125th @ f/4 (full aperture) with ISO set to 200 with your kit lens, that will be fine for a static shot. For an action shot, you'll need a minimum of /500th to stop subject movement. You can't open the lens up any more to let in more light. What you can do is set the **ISO** to 800. That will give you your desired 1/500th@f/4. As ever with life there are no free lunches. To raise the sensor's sensitivity to light, it simply amplifies the signal. This amplifies any noise present too, which takes a grainy form of random coloured dots. You have to decide for yourself how much noise you can tolerate in order to get the exposure settings you need. I happily use up to 6400 **ISO** without concern. You can reduce noise in post processing to some extent, at the cost of detail. **Note:** this button has two raised dots on it so that you can locate it (and therefore the buttons left and right of it) by touch

• 12 The **Exposure Compensation** button. The light metering system of the S1 is highly sophisticated and rarely wrong footed but it can happen. Sometimes, for pictorial reasons you want a lighter or darker result than the 'correct' exposure gives. In a snow scene, for example, the camera will tend to underexpose, rendering the snow grey rather than white. Good as it is, no auto exposure system is perfect. A press on this button brings up a +/- scale so that you can set the compensation that you judge necessary. I rarely find the exposure needs tweaking beyond + or - 2/3. One of the greatest assets of the **EVF** is that you can see live the effect of any compensation you make. Ultimately, although we think in terms of correct and incorrect exposure, the lightness or darkness of an image is an artistic choice

• 13 The power switch. About the only thing on the S1 that isn't customizable.

• 14 The **Rear Dial**. This has different functions according to which Mode, A, S etc is chosen and is a key control during picture taking. If you are in **A** mode, for example, it will change the aperture, in **S** mode the shutter speed. Some aspects of its operation can be tailored in **Custom→Operation→Dial Set.** in the Custom menu

• 15 The **Status-LCD** lighting switch. Turns on illumination of the LCD and several buttons for easier operation of the S1 in dark conditions. You can tailor levels of illumination etc in

Setup→Monitor/Display→Status-LCD

• 16 The **LCD Status** panel. This gives an immediate view of all the things you need to know about the S1 during shooting. White Balance, Metering Mode, Aperture, ISO, Shutter speed, card slots in use, battery status including battery grip if in use, exposure compensation, quality and picture size. Plus how many shots you have left at the current setting or time for video. It can be a battery saver if you find you can do without the monitor for checking shooting information

• 17 The **AF ON** button. This overrides any focus setting and always focuses the camera when pushed. So,even if in **MF**, press this and the S1 will focus. This can be used for what is known as back button focusing, much used by sports photographers. Set the **Focus Mode** to AFC. Switch off

Custom→Focus/Shutter£rarr;Shutter AF. Now the camera will only focus when the **AF ON** is pushed. All the time you want to track a subject, keep the button pressed and the S1 will keep them in focus. If someone much closer gets between you and your subject momentarily, leave go the button. This will prevent the camera moving focus to the near obstruction and having to make a big focus adjustment, only to have to readjust when the coast is clear. So, when you press the button again, focus will resume where you left off. It gives you direct and instantaneous control over your focusing. In **Custom→Fn Button Set→Setting in REC mode→AF-ON** you can bias the focusing towards **Near** or **Far** subjects if you wish. This bias only takes effect when focusing via the **AF-ON** button. If you focus using a half press of the shutter, no matter the **AF-ON** setting, focus will be ascertained by the standard unbiased method. The bias only applies to focusing methods using the grid pattern, not to Pinpoint etc where the user explicitly tells the camera where to focus..

• 18 The **Joystick**. This puts the positioning of the **AF Area** under instant and intuitive control. Nudge it and the **AF Area** moves smoothly up, down or diagonally to any extreme of the frame. A half touch on the shutter button will set its position to wherever you have moved it. A press on the **Joystick** will move the **AF Area** back to dead centre. Another press will return to the previously set position and toggles between them. Not only that but while the **AF Area** is highlighted, turning the **Rear Dial** will alter its size. You can reassign the **Joystick** as a function button, for menu operation or even disable it if you wish. I don't think you will, though!

• 19 The **AF Mode** button. The **AF Mode** is critical to getting the best results from the S1. While you can tweak exposure in post processing, you can't make a fuzzy sharp. The S1 has 8 modes to choose from and it is important to use an appropriate one for the the photography being undertaken. For that reason, I am giving a detailed rundown on each of the at the end of this section, after item 23

• 20 The **Focus Mode** lever. **S**, Single Autofocus, means when you half press the shutter button, the camera focuses and does not focus again until you again half press the shutter button or press the **AF ON** button. **C** is Continuous Autofocus. All the time you keep the shutter button half pressed the camera will attempt to keep the subject in focus. If the subject is moving fast, the S1 will predict where the subject will be when the shutter fires. **M** is manual focus where you turn the lens focus ring and judge sharp focus for yourself. This is of use on the rare occasions the S1 cannot find focus for itself. Generally speaking, the camera's auto focus will be faster and more accurate than your eyes. **Focus Modes** work hand in glove with the **Drive Mode**, **S** for single shots, **C** for **H M** and **L Burst** rates

• 21 The **Rec** button. Press this at any time and the camera will start shooting a video using the default settings you have made in the **Motion Picture** menu. To gain full access to video parameters you must set the **Mode Dial** to **Creative Video**

• 22 The Viewfinder/ Monitor switching sensor

• 23 The viewfinder dioptre adjustment wheel (hidden from view). Set it for maximum sharpness when looking at the viewfinder information or a detailed scene

AF Modes

Note: By default not all of the **AF Modes** are shown. I show them all in the listing below. You can show

or hide any of the **AF Modes** in
Custom→Focus/Shutter 1→Show/Hide AF Mode
• **Face/Eye/Body/Animal Detection (Fig 07)** will
recognise beings or parts of them and set focus
accordingly. When several qualifying subjects are
identified, white frames are placed around them so that
you can select the one on which you wish to focus bu
touching the monitor. Also, each half press of the
shutter will scroll though the boxes, though I find this a
little eccentric in operation. When a face is identified
and the subject of focus you will see a cross hair in the
box on the eye nearest the camera. Ideal for
portraiture,It effectively removes the need for you to
worry about focusing at all, leaving you free to
concentrate on your subject. You can switch off
Animal Detection by pressing the **Up** Cursor key, at
which the icon changes to **Animal Detection Disabled
(Fig 08) Note:** you can move the selected area around
with the Cursor Keys or Joystick and vary the size with
the Front and Rear Dials
• **Tracking (Fig 09)** will attempt to follow whatever
you set it to follow and keep focus on it. This works
with **AFC** only. It works remarkably well. Just touch
whatever you want to keep in focus on the screen, half
press the shutter button and the S1 will track it from
there. It sounds like the perfect focus method but if
your subject goes out of frame for a moment or turns
around or something comes between the camera and
them, **Tracking** is lost. Particularly good, therefore for
a subject that will move around in a set space and will
not be obstructed. I find it good for shooting bands in
low light at wide apertures, where I can track the
singers face accurately in spite of limited depth of field

as he or she moves around the mic. **Note:** when **Tracking** is lost, the focus area turns red. To resume, put the focus area where you want to track and half press the shutter as before.

• **225 Area (Fig 10)** monitors the whole screen and puts focus at the most likely spot. Panasonic's algorithm for doing this is one of the best and it can be uncannily accurate. It indicates where it will focus - multiple boxes mean that all those points are at the same distance from the camera and will thus be in focus. **Note:** If you are shooting in **AFC** you can, if you wish, set the point at which focus will commence. It's a bit involved but if you need it, go to **Custom→Focus/Shutter2→AFC Start Point (225-Area) (Fig 14)** and set it **On**. Now the icon will change to **225-Area Start Point** and a cross will appear on the screen. Move it where you wish and that is where **AFC** will look first to set its focus area. If you were photographing a runner, say, entering your field of view from the right and running diagonally across the frame area to exit on your left, set the cross to the right where they enter your field of view and half press the shutter. **AFC** will pick them up and follow from there.

•**Zone (Vert./Horz.)(Fig 11)** This and **Square** and **Oval** following are essentially crops of the **225-Area**. You can change the position and/or orientation of the **Zone** via the Cursor keys or Joystick. You can alter the size of the **Zone** with the rear dial. You can also alter the size by pinching the **Zone**, though I find this less convenient. While highlighted in yellow, the **Zone** can be reset to centre at any time by pressing the **Disp.** button

•**Zone (Square) (Fig 12)**
• **Zone (Oval) (Fig 13)**
•**1-Area+ (Fig 15)** This is a more flexible version of the most basic **AF Mode, 1-Area**. As with **1-Area** you need to keep the focus area over the part of the subject you want in focus. The beauty of **1-Area** is that you are telling the S1 within close confines where you want to focus. Rather than use processing power working out the best place to focus within a wider area, it can lock straight on, using all its processing power to do so. The downside of **1-Area** is that with anything other than a static subject, it can be tricky to keep the focus area right on target. **1-Area+** addresses this by taking into account an area immediately outside the focus box indicated by corner brackets. This area will expand or contract as necessary if you change the size of the **AF Area**

• **1-Area (Fig 16)** is my standard setting. I find it the most certain and controllable and very quick to focus on my subject. I find one size up from the smallest gives the camera a decent area to lock on to. At the smallest it is easy to find the camera hunting while trying to focus on a small blank subject area. Old habits die hard and I still find placing **1-Area** on the subject, half pressing the shutter to lock focus and then re-composing, quicker than shifting the **AF Area** around the screen with the **Joystick**

• **Pinpoint (Fig 17)** is great for macro mode or anywhere where you need a really precise positional focusing. It automatically enlarges the view so that you can set the cross hairs very precisely. Useful when, for example, you are photographing an animal behind bars in a zoo. **Pinpoint** enables you to reliably focus between the bars

•**Custom 1-3 (Fig 18)** enables you to set any focus area pattern you like. For a cyclist approaching you head on, an area 6 squares wide by 1 tall 2/3rds of the way up the screen might be useful to obviate the danger of focus transferring to the background or to another cyclist to the left or right. It's easy to set up. Press **AF Mode** button and select **Custom 1**, say. Now press the **Up** cursor and you will see a grid covering most of the screen. Just touch the boxes on the screen to define the focusing area you want. The boxes will fill in yellow. Pressing **Disp.** will clear all the boxes at any time. Alternatively, after pressing the **Up** cursor key, move the + sign in the middle box where you want and press **Menu/Set**. That will toggle the selected box on or off. When you are satisfied with the area, press the **Q** button to set the area. Try it out and if you are happy, go back to the **Custom 1** setting you just altered and press **Save**. That is now your **Custom 1** focus area setting

The Rear Panel

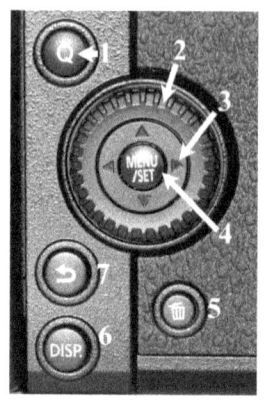

• 1 The Q **button** This provides fast access to often used settings in a special, customizable menu. It can be configured separately for stills and video

• 2 The **Control Dial**. This is a versatile control which when turned will scroll though whatever parameter you are accessing on screen. Push the **ISO** button and this dial will run through the settings, for example. Or you can use it to control the volume of headphones. Its function can be changed in **Custom→Operation 2→Dial Set.**

• 3 The **Cursor Keys**. Press the **Control Dial** where indicated and the dial acts like the arrow or cursor keys on other models.

• 4 The **Menu/Set** button. It is basic to the operation of the S1, accesses the menu, sets and confirms the menu options and is used throughout the camera's operation for setting and confirming actions.

• 5 The **Delete** button is used to delete images in **Playback** mode. Press the **AF Mode** button to toggle between Card slots 1 and 2

• 6 The **Disp.** button. For the EVF this toggles between two screen views, one with minimal information the other comprehensive information. For the Monitor only it can cycle through those 2 screens but with the option of 2 more, **Monitor Off** and **Control Panel**, set in **Custom→Monitor/Display 3→Show/Hide Monitor Layout**. A useful item is the **Fn** with spanner icon. Touch this and a guide to all of your Button settings comes up. Useful because they are easily forgotten. You can alter them here too.

• 7 The **Cancel** button Does what it says, backs up through menu settings and acts a bit like the Esc. key on a PC

The Front Panel

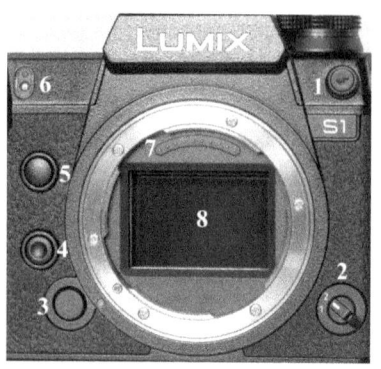

• 1 The **Flash Synchro** socket. This simply triggers an external flash via a lead. It has no automatic functions at all. You could use it for studio flash or for older flashes.

• 2 The **Fn Lever** I find this useful for an important setting because it is easy to find and easy to feel which position it is in. For that reason I set it to switch between **MECH.** and **ELEC.** shutters. You use **Function of Fn Lever** to set the overall action and then the **Mode 2 Setting** to set which of those choices available should be invoked by the **..** (up) position. **Custom→Fn Lever Setting** takes you to the wide range of choices available

• 3 The **Lens Release** button. You need to press this before turning the lens to remove it from the S1

• 4 The **Fn2** function button. By default it is set to **Preview** which allows you to see the effect of stopping the lens down on depth of field and with another press the effect of your shutter speed as well

• 5 The Fn1 **button**. There are more than 60 functions to which the button can be set so you should find something useful!

• 6 The **Lamp**. It flashes to tell you when the **Self-Timer** is about to fire the shutter. It also function as

the **Function Assist Lamp** which throws out a beam
of light to aid autofocus when the light is very dim. If
you use the camera in **Silent Mode** the lamp will be
turned off automatically. You can set it on or off in
Photo→Focus→AF Assist Light

• 7 The **electrical contacts**. These are aligned with the
contacts on the rear of the lens and transmit data
between lens and camera for focusing, stabilization etc.
It's a good idea to give them an occasional wipe over
with a lint free cloth

• 8 The **image sensor**. The sensor itself is covered by a
glass protection layer so that anything that gets into the
camera cannot damage the sensor itself. Inevitably
specks of dust and foreign matter will find their way
on to the glass. They make their presence known only
when the lens is stopped down past f/11 or so. What
you actually see is the shadow of the dust on the
sensor. The S1 goes through a cleaning routine very
time you turn it on which gets rid of most specks of
dust. If the dust persists, it can usually be dislodged
with a 'rocket' style hand operated air blower. No high
pressure jets of air or air cans! Avoid changing lenses
in sandy or dusty environments where possible. It's a
good idea to hold the S1 face down when making a
lens change so that dust does not fall on to it while it is
exposed.

Photo Menu - Image Quality 1

Photo Style

This gives you a series of preset colour values other than the standard neutral output. Each can be customized with regard to **Contrast**, **Sharpness**, **Noise Reduction** and **Saturation**. I find all the default 0 settings good for my purposes except for **Noise Reduction** which at 0 is too aggressive for my taste. I set it to -5 since I am willing to accept some noise in return for maintaining sharpness. **Note:** Settings here apply to both stills and video, so if you set **Cinelike D** while shooting a movie, don't forget to re-set the **Style** before shooting stills.

Standard

Plain vanilla neutral values and the pick for general use.

Vivid

This is self-explanatory though I'd have called it Lurid.

Natural

Gives pleasantly soft colours.

Flat

Lowish contrast with almost pastel colours, it can look rather stylish with the right subjects.

Landscape

Souped up blues and greens.

Portrait

Warms the skin tones.

Monochrome

Black and white! When this is set a new option appear on the right of the screen. It allows you to select red, green, yellow or orange filters. These are the classic filters used in film days with red being the most dramatic, yielding dark, almost black skies that enhance the dramatic effect of any clouds. You can also add grain effects.

L.Monochrome

This is a nice gutsy black and white, great for moody landscapes. Do try the filters with this one!

L.Monochrome D

This is an even more gutsy monochrome for those gritty urban landscapes.

Cinelike D

This is mainly used by video makers but you may like it for stills. It is flat in contrast and is intended to use as much of the dynamic range of the sensor as possible, retaining the maximum detail in the shadows and highlights. Then, for post processing you can tailor the image to your liking. For stills, if you are going to this much trouble, you might as well shoot **RAW** which retains everything the sensor records and offers you maximum flexibility on post processing.

Cinelike V

Like the previous entry, this is mainly for video use. It is intended to give film like images which to my eyes looks quite like **Standard** but with slightly denser colours, somewhere between **Standard** and **Vivid**.

Like709

Video again. If you understand this highly technical setting, you probably don't need this book! Rec 709 is a colour standard used for high definition broadcasting. It is identical to sRGB. High end cameras have a wider gamut, or colour range than that, so Like709 is is designed to retain the whole gamut of the S1 by compressing the brightest areas to fit the monitor. You can then colour manage it in post precessing to get the result you want on your monitor. There's always the problem that it will look different on other monitors unless they are colour managed but there is little you can do about that.

Knee

This lets you choose the brightness point at which highlight compression will start (Point)and the fierceness (Slope) of the compression.

MY PHOTO STYLE 1-4

Here you can set the S1 to record JPGs to your own specification in terms of contrast, sharpness, noise reduction, saturation (the intensity of the colours) and hue, the colours themselves. So, for example, if **Vivid** was not vivid enough you up the contrast and saturation sliders and save that as **My Photo Style 1**. You can change the name to a more memorable one by pressing **Edit** when saving. You need to experiment with these to see what you prefer. The styles do not affect **RAW** files but if you set **RAW+JPG** you get a normal **RAW** plus the styled **JPG**, effectively giving you the best of both worlds.**Note:** if you shoot in **HLG Photo** mode, the Photo Styles are limited to **Standard (HLG)** or **Monochrome (HLG)**. You will need a suitable TV to view these images.

Metering Mode

This sets the way in which the camera reads the light falling on your picture. This setting applies to both stills and video.

Multiple (Fig 19)

The whole screen is read and the camera judges the exposure for you. In my experience the **Multiple** setting is very reliable and even when it does err it is not by very much.

Center Weighted (Fig 20)

Weights the exposure to the centre of the screen on the reasonable assumption that that is where the subject is. It was a method used by film cameras and remains for legacy reasons more than anything else. In practice **Multiple** does everything **Center Weighted** does but better and more intelligently. Although consider **Highlight Weighted** as well.

Spot (Fig 21)

Measures the exposure from the centre of the screen. A small green cross appears on the screen to tell you it is spot metering. This works best when the lighting is extreme. For example, you are photographing a bird sitting on a telephone wire with a bright blue sky behind it. The camera on **Multiple** will try to set a compromise exposure by balancing the bird with blue sky light reading. It cannot know that you care only for getting detail in the bird's plumage. Set to **Spot** and it will expose for the bird. This metering mode can be tricky, requiring experience to use. In a situation as outlined, I prefer to use **Exposure Compensation** to add a stop or so or otherwise use the **Auto Bracket** setting.

Highlight Weighted (Fig 22)

There are many occasions where you find yourself photographing something light in dark surroundings. An example would be a singer on stage wearing a light coloured outfit and lit by a spotlight. Under these circumstances even the sophisticated **Multi-**

Metering will read the whole scene and instead of setting exposure for the singer, set it for the overall darker picture, leading to the subject being overexposed. **Highlight Weighted** tells the S1 to major on the highlight exposure giving you full tonal range on the singer. You could use **Center Weighted** but this is pretty crude compared to **Highlight Weighted** and, of course your subject may well not be in the center of the frame.

Aspect Ratio
4:3

This is a useful ratio for specialized photo monitors and printing, being the same ratio as 8x6 and 16x12 standard printing paper. It is less important these days when A4 and A3 formats are often used for printing. The native format of the S1 is 3:2 (below) which yields the greatest file size.

3:2

is the old 35mm film camera ratio and the most effective use of the S1's sensor for stills pictures, yielding the largest file size and pixel count. Any **RAW** files shot will be in this aspect ratio, all other ratios being a crop of this one. Thus, **3:2** gives 8368x5584 pixels while **4:3** crops that to 7440x5584 pixels, giving a slightly narrower horizontal angle of view.

16:9

is widescreen TV/ Video aspect.

1:1

is the aspect of many older film cameras, usually 6x6cm in size and used by such cameras as Rolleiflex and Hasselblad. It is a rather awkward shape for most pictures but there are those who like it. It gives only a 14.5M image as compared to 20M at **4:3** since it crops the image to 3888x 3888. With **3:2** and **16:9** the S1 is simply cropping the top and bottom sensor image to get the ratio required and the pixel width of the image will always be the same at 5184 pixels. You could argue that it would be better to shoot always at **4:3** and the crop out any unwanted image areas but it is much easier in practise to view and compose the picture in the aspect ratio you have chosen.

65:24 and 2:1

These are convenient aspect ratios for shooting panoramas. There's no built in panorama function on the S1 so it needs to be done manually with overlapping frames, ideally on a tripod. **Note:** The **Panoramic** aspect ratios, **16:9** and **1:1** are not compatible with many special modes of operation of the S1 like **High Resolution**. If you find you can't access them, simply make sure you are not using a special mode. A lot of problems can be solved by having a **Custom** or **Saved** setting that puts the camera in a plain vanilla shooting setup. If something is greyed out, you can go to this setting and it should be available.

Picture Quality

The two basic choices for digital cameras are always **RAW** or **JPG**. A rough analogy could be between a negative and a print in film photography. **RAW** would be the negative in that it is simply the information captured via the lens onto the sensor. It is a sobering though that your masterpiece in the **RAW** consists only of a massively long series of **0**s and **1**s. It only becomes the photo you envisaged after a complex processing sequence. You cannot view a **RAW** without the S1 first processing it to a **JPG**. So, if you shoot a **RAW** frame, what you view on the monitor is not the **RAW** file itself but a smallish **JPG** which the S1 processed and embedded in the **RAW** image as it was recorded. That is also what you will be viewing when you copy a **RAW** file to your computer/tablet/ phone. You can in fact process the **RAW** file into a **JPG** in **Playback→Process Image→RAW Processing** if you wish, though most will prefer to do it in a suitable image editing program on their computer. The **JPG** is analogous to a photographic print. It is the digital information from the S1s sensor processed into a viewable, editable and usable picture. If you decided you wanted a monochrome version of your picture, you would simply discard the colour information from the **RAW** file, for example. This throws into relief the difference between shooting **RAW** and shooting **JPG**. If you set the S1 to shoot **JPG** and set it to a monochrome **Photo Style**, the camera shoots the picture, extracts the monochrome information necessary, produces the **JPG** and discards the **RAW** data. Once done, if you decide you would prefer a colour rendition of the scene, you cannot have it because you have discarded that information. Had you shot **RAW**, you could extract the just monochrome information for your monochrome pic but if you didn't like it, make another **JPG** this time using the colour information. This is putting the difference in the most extreme way for purposes of illustration. here is a rundown of the most salient differences.

RAW (pro)

• Retains all the information captured by the sensor at the maximum size of the sensor

• Can produce any size, quality, style of **JPG** at any time you choose

• If some radical new image processing algorithm, noise reducing software, for example, is invented you can apply it to **RAW** images taken years ago

RAW Con

• Large file sizes

• Requires post processing to do anything other than view a small preview (though the previw is fine for viewing on a tablet, in Lightroom etc

JPG Pro

• Smaller file sizes

• Can be recorded in a variety of sizes and aspect ratios

• Viewable and usable immediately in full size and with no further processing

JPG Con

• loss of detail (though with lesser rates of compression this is practically unnoticeable)

• Fewer colours than **RAW** since **JPG** is recorded at 8-bit depth rather than 14. The extra bit depth is of more use to give greater scope for post processing than for viewing since the **JPG**'s 8-bit gives nearly 17 million colours while the normal human eye can distinguish around 10 million.

• Lower dynamic range, meaning it cannot record the brightness range that **RAW** can. With **RAW**, if your image is under or over-exposed you can lighten or darken it at least 2 stops in post processing. With **JPG** most of that extra highlight or shadow detail is discarded when the **JPG** is cooked.

Note: the obvious answer to the **RAW/JPG** question is to shoot both at the same time. Otherwise it is horses for courses. For family and social media shots, **JPG** is just fine. I personally prefer to shoot **Large/ Fine JPG**s because once while I can discard detail from large file, I can't reclaim it from a small one. Having said that, the smallest files with highest compression work just fine for social media. **RAW** is best for those exhibition shots or for framing where you want the absolute best, sharpest and most dynamic result the S1 can do.

Picture Size

Note: This applies to the JPG files only. If you are shooting **RAW** only, this will be blanked out because **RAW** always uses the full sensor area. **Picture Size** sets the number of Megapixels or MP your camera will record from the sensor when you are shooting **RAW+JPG** or **JPG** alone. As previously noted, the **RAW** file will be 8368x5584px whatever the JPG setting.

L(arge), M(edium, S(mall)

For Each **Aspect ratio** (see previous entry) you are offered a choice of **L**, **M** or **S** image sizes. Each of these roughly halves the file size of the previous one, hence **3:2 L** gives 46., **3:2 M** gives 23M and **3:2 S** 12M. If you are using APS-C lenses, the principle applies but all the sizes will be smaller pro rata, of course. For many applications, the **S** setting would be more than enough but it needs to be borne in mind that the smaller file sizes are obtained at the cost of image detail. While you discard image detail from a

L file, you can't add it back in from **M** or **S**. The smaller file sizes can be useful if you are transmitting your pictures over the Internet or they are for social media use. They used to be handy for saving in storage space but given the low cost of storage media nowadays, the savings are less important.

HLG Photo

This stands for Hybrid Log Gamma. It's a form of High Dynamic Range (**HDR**), that is it encompasses a wider range of dark to light than the standard dynamic range. The problem with **HDR** is that when viewed on a non **HDR** monitor or screen, it looks rather flat, lacking in contrast. **HLG** gets around that by encoding both standard dynamic range and **HDR** together - hence the '**Hybrid**'. Thus, it will look OK on any screen, standard or **HDR**. **Note:** neither the S1's **EVF** or monitor can display a High Dynamic Range and images with **HLG** on look very dark. Images must be output via the S1's **HDMI** plug to an **HLG** enabled TV for the effect to show. **Note:** in the past this has been seen as a video parameter but Panasonic see it as being just as useful for stills, so a degree of future proofing here.. HLG won't work with the two panoramic **Aspect Ratios**.

Full-Res

It's not actually the full resolution of the camera but not far short and varies according to the **Aspect Ratio** set.

4K-Res.

Records at true **4K**, 3840x2160 in 16:9 **Aspect Ratio** and a bit less in the others. This would be more than enough for an **FHD** or **4K** TV or monitor.

High Resolution Mode

The S1's body stabilization system works by moving the sensor in the opposite direction to the movement of the camera in your hands. This system is used to provide higher resolution by taking a series of pictures with the sensor shifted very slightly between each one and then merging them. This takes longer to do than making one exposure and for that reason, the camera should be on tripod or firm mount and the subject static.

Start

After setting the parameters below, touch this. You will see the **High Resolution icon (Fig 23)** on the left of the monitor (it flashes at first). Pressing the shutter button after this will record in **High Resolution** mode. When you have finished, you return to normal resolution by pressing the **Q** button on the back of the S1. The icon will disappear.

Simul Record Normal Shot

Regardless of the **Picture Quality** setting This gives you 2 RAW images, one at the sensor's normal full resolution and another in **High Resolution**, 12000x8000 for the 3:2 **Aspect Ratio**.

Shutter Delay

Because the camera needs to be still for **High Resolution** mode, it is wise to set a delay between pressing the shutter button and the shutter firing to give any movement caused a chance to settle down. 2 or 4 seconds usually enough.

Motion Blur Processing

Sometimes it cannot be guaranteed that a subject shows no movement. In a landscape, the leaves on the trees, for example. The S1 has two ways of dealing with this.

• **Mode 1** - the camera gives full resolution but any movement will be seen as blur in the image and potentially spoil it

• **Mode 2** - the camera attempts to correct for any movement. In doing so, it will take information from any one of the six frames shot which is sharp. This drops part of the merging process and so compromises the resolution

Note: this mode produces files of almost 200MB size so you will need a pretty powerful computer to handle them. It always uses the electronic shutter so there is no shake of the camera when it fires. Thus it is useful to fire the camera from your phone using the Lumix Sync app for the S1 so that no shutter delay is necessary. ISO is restricted to 3200 and you can only use Single or Manual AF.

Long Exposure NR

Removes noise from frames taken at long shutter speeds, night scenes, for example. In low light and at long exposures the image sensor generates noise of its own. **Long Exposure NR** very effectively lowers that noise but due to the way it operates doubles the time for capture of an image. If you have an exposure time of 10 seconds, the camera will be processing for 10 seconds after the exposure. I would never turn this off unless I really had to. It works by taking a second reading of the sensor with the same exposure length after your picture and looking to see where noise has been generated. It then subtracts that noise from your picture, cleaning it up. **Note:** It will

be greyed out if you are using the electronic shutter
since that cannot make long exposures.

Photo Menu - Image Quality 2

ISO Sensitivity (photo)

This sets the minimum and maximum **ISO** settings
that the S1 can choose when set to **ISO Auto**. It is
likely that you will find an **ISO** setting where the
noise is too high for your taste. If it is **ISO** 12800,
then setting **ISO Auto Upper Limit Setting** to 6400
will prevent the camera from straying that far
upwards when set to **Auto**. Similarly, if you find that
you prefer to use high shutter speeds, setting **ISO
Auto Lower Limit Setting** to, **ISO** 800 will keep
the shutter speed up. I find a lower setting of 100 and
a higher one of 6400 keeps the image quality within
acceptable bounds for my work. If you want to use a
ISO 12800 or more, you can set it manually
whatever the upper or lower limits you set here.

Min shutter Speed

This tells the S1 the lowest shutter speed it can
select when **ISO Auto** is set. You might set this to
1/500th for sport or 1/10th (given the excellent
stabilization of the S1 and lenses) for night shots.
Your setting here is not an absolute, however. If the
camera is using the maximum **ISO** you have set in
ISO Sensitivity (photo) above and the lens is
already at its maximum aperture, it will maintain
correct exposure by using a lower shutter speed
anyway.

i.Dynamic Range

If the S1 senses that the brightness range of the
scene is greater than the camera can handle, it will
manipulate the exposure and contrast settings of the

camera to compensate. Something to try if a scene is obviously problematic, a pic of a room interior with a window in shot or heavily backlit portrait, maybe. Such situations can be handled better by **HLG** (see Image Quality 1 menu) but you will need a compatible display to get the benefit. Otherwise, there is **HDR** (High dynamic Range) which you would have to implement in post processing. Take a series of exposures, one at normal exposure then plus 1, plus 2, -1,-2 stops. Most imaging software will have an automatic **HDR** function. The trouble with **HDR** is that it has a tendency to make the image look flat and dull. The inescapable fact is that if you have an image with a dynamic range beyond what your monitor can display, there will always be some compromise necessary. **HLG** helps by only letting you see the full range on a screen that can display it.

Vignetting Comp

 Many lenses, especially wide-angles exhibit a darkening at the periphery of the image, sometimes a stop or more darker than the centre. In most pictures, it doesn't matter and looks perfectly natural, part of the varying brightness of the scene. Sometimes, though, when the image has large areas of even colouring, it looks uncomfortably like an old fashioned vignette mask has been applied.

Vignetting Comp boosts the **ISO** in those darkened areas, thus evening them up. Unfortunately, that can increase the noise in the boosted areas and since noise shows most on expanses of even brightness, this i=s not something to leave on all the time. With native lenses for the S1, any vignetting is mild and rarely objectionable.

Diffraction Compensation

When you pass light through a very small hole it bends it. This is known as diffraction. When you stop a lens down to a small aperture, say f/11 and beyond, the aperture (or diaphragm) becomes small enough to diffract some of the focused light of your image. This causes the image to look 'soft' or slightly blurred. It is an optical phenomenon and nothing can be done about it except to apply extra sharpening to the image which is what **Diffraction Compensation** seems to do. While it improves the apparent sharpness, as with any digital sharpening it can highlight noise in the image. **Diffraction Compensation** is subtly implemented on the S1 and well worth leaving at **Auto** when shooting subjects which require great depth of field and thus a smaller aperture.

Filter Settings

Filter Effect

Make your choice from the 22 **effects** available. Some effects have a changeable component and for many of them it is easiest to operate with **Touch Tab** in **Touch Settings** in the **Custom** menu turned on. With all of the filters, pressing the **WB** button brings up the basic adjustment. Some are more complicated; **One Point Color**, for example. To choose the colour to retain, touch the **Dropper Icon (Fig 24)** and then touch the colour required. Having done that, turn the rear dial to set its intensity. If you prefer you can enter the settings screen by touching the control dial in the Up (12 o/c) position.

Simultaneous Record W/O Filter

This is a useful facility which is only available when **Quality** is set to **JPG**. One press on the shutter makes 2 pictures, one with the filter in operation and one without so if the effect doesn't look good you haven't lost your picture. Note: If you load both filtered and unfiltered images into layers in Photoshop (or any image program with layers) you can blend the two, making the effect more subtle. If you are in **Burst Mode** or **Auto Bracket** when you set a filter, your S1 will revert to single shot. **Note:** a quirk here is that if you have the camera set to shoot a **RAW** frame, the **RAW** file will show the **Filter** applied on the monitor. If you import the **RAW** file into an image editor, tough,you will find that it is not applied. It shouldn't be, of course. **RAW** means the stream of binary generated by the sensor. If you could alter it it would no longer be a **RAW** file. The reason you see it is that every **RAW** file has a smallish **JPG** image embedded in it, purely for viewing purposes.

Photo Menu - Focus

AF Custom Setting(Photo)

This applies only to **AFC** operation. It enables you to set tweak **AFC** settings to suit the movement of your subject. The settings 1 to 4 cover a wide range of movement types and are well chosen and set up,as you'd expect. I'd love to offer advice here I just use **Set 1** generally, since I find that if I'm photographing a rugby game, say, the player may be running towards me, then weaving and running in and out of the pack and then just weaving. It really isn't possible to change to the ideal setting for every change of movement! Tweaking the factory settings would need to be done in the light of experience and experimentation. On the other hand, if you are photographing racing cars from a fixed position trackside, it would be well worth using **Set 2** and turning **AF Sensitivity** down a little.

AF Assist Light

Switched **ON**, in low light where the camera might have difficulty establishing focus, a surprisingly bright red light comes on just long enough for the camera to lock on. Although the S1 will focus in very low light, it does have its limits. If you switch to **Silent Mode**, the S1 assumes that you will not wish to draw attention to yourself and switches the light off automatically.

Focus Peaking

is a focusing aid that works with manual focus. It gives a graphic representation of which areas of your picture are sharply focused by highlighting the edges. It comes into its own in poor lighting when judging focus by eye is difficult.

Focus Peaking Sensitivity

-2 represents the most precise setting, +2 the least. The higher the setting the more boldly outlined the in-focus areas will be and the less precise the focus. It thus require a bigger turn pf the focusing ring to make it appear or disappear. At lower setting, the outlining is thinner and more precise, a smaller turn of the focus ring making it appear or vanish. For general purposes, the mid setting is probably best. For video, if the peaking outline is too thick it can interfere with your view of the action.

Display Color

Choose the colour of your peak outlining.

Display While AFS

Normally **Focus Peaking** only operates when using **Manual Focus**, since autofocus requires no input from the camera operator to find focus.. However, switch this on and when you half-press the shutter button, the peaking appears. You can use it to confirm that the S1 is focusing where you want. It can also be handy if you have **AF+MF** in the **Custom** menu set on. (This allows you to manually alter the camera's focus while using **AFS**.

1-Area AF Moving Speed

If you are shooting in **AF Mode**s **1-Area**, **1-Area+** or **Face/Eye/Body/Animal Detect.**, this allows you to change the speed with which the yellow outlined**Focus Area** box moves around the screen when you use the **Joystick** or **Cursor Buttons**.

Photo Menu - Flash 1

Flash Mode

Forced On (Fig 25)

The flash fires regardless of lighting conditions. The shutter speed can be set up to 1/250th sec. Handy for backlit sunlight portraits for example. You will actually see two flashes, the first, less strong one being the pilot flash for the camera/ flash to judge the exposure necessary.

Forced On/Red-Eye (Fig 26)

The flash fires regardless of lighting conditions as in the first option but fires a couple of pre-flashes to reduce red-eye.

Slow Sync.(Fig 27)

This is effective to balance flash on a foreground subject with natural light on the background. Usually, you'll need to mount the camera on a tripod for this as it will often need slow shutter speeds. If you are photographing someone or something in a darkish room in **A** mode with an ambient light level of 1/15th @ f/2.8, with normal flash sync, the shutter speed will not drop below 1/60th. Your subject, in the foreground will be correctly lit by the flash but the background will be dark. With **Slow Sync** set, the shutter speed will drop to the required 1/15th so that both the subject and background will be correctly exposed. **Note:** With this setting, the shutter speed will be allowed to rise above the 1/250th maximum that camera can sync to the flash. In this case, the flash simply doesn't fire.

Slow Sync./Red-Eye) (Fig 28)

Slow sync. with red-eye reduction.

Forced Flash Off (Fig 29)

This disables the flash regardless of any other settings. A use for this would be for a wedding photographer, for example. Set the **Flash Mode** to a function button so that if you are photographing outside using fill-in flash to lighten shadows but flash is forbidden in the church you can have peace of mind of knowing that even if left on, the flash will not fire.

<u>Firing Mode</u>

This will normally be greyed out. It applies only to flashes that are powered from the camera battery rather than having their own. They were supplied with some earlier models. The choices are **TTL** where you camera sets the flash output automatically or **Manual** where you control it yourself using **Manual Flash Adjust** below.

<u>Flash Adjust</u>

If you find your picture under or overexposed when shooting in **TTL** mode, you can correct it three stops either way from here.

<u>Flash Synchro</u>

This sets whether the flash fires at the beginning or end of the exposure. It doesn't make any difference at normally used shorter flash sync shutter speeds, 1/60th and upwards, where your exposure is made by the light emanating from the flash. At lower speeds, though, you will probably pick up some of the ambient light which will be mixed with the flash light. If you have a moving subject, this gives a sharp image from the flash light and a blurred one from the ambient light. It is an interesting and versatile artistic resource.

1st

This is the normal setting. If the exposure is 1 second, for example, the flash will fire at the beginning of the exposure and any blur will appear to be in front of the moving object. This will look rather odd - and interesting.

2nd

The flash will fire just before the shutter closes, motion blur will be appear behind the moving object and give the effect of speed.

Manual Flash Adjust

This will normally be greyed out. It is for use with legacy flashes powered from the camera battery rather than the flash as is usual.

Auto Exposure Comp

This applies only when using flash. With this **Off**, any **Exposure Compensation (Fig 30)** set will affect only the ambient light. Set **On** both ambient light and flash level will be changed. If have a subject in a dimly lit room and you want the room to be lighter in comparison to the subject, leave this **Off**. Now, if you set the **Exposure Compensation** +1 stop, the room will be one stop brighter but your subject remains the same. If you feel your overall exposure is too dark or light set this **On** and the overall image will be lightened or darkened.

Red-Eye Removal

when the flash is set to either of the red-eye reduction settings **(Fig 31 and 32)**, if the camera

detects any residual red-eye it corrects it
automatically.

Wireless

 You can use a flash in the S1's hot shoe to trigger a
remote flash or flashes. This is called wireless flash.
When set **On** the items in the next menu **Flash 2**
become available. Otherwise they are greyed out.

Photo Menu - Flash 2

Wireless Channel

Wireless Channel If you are using a wireless flash it will have 4 operating channels. You set the remote flash and camera to the same channel. Wireless FP With certain wireless flashes this makes possible the use of a higher shutter speed than the 250th second of a standard camera flash. The reason you cannot use a faster shutter speed than 1/250th with flash normally is that the flash pulse time is shorter than the time it takes the shutter to travel across the sensor. Therefore only a narrow band across of the subject shows as lit by the flash. **FP** works by firing a series of flash pulses in rapid succession.

Wireless FP

With certain wireless flashes this makes possible the use of a higher shutter speed than the 1/320th second of a standard camera flash. The reason you cannot use a faster shutter speed than 1/320th with flash normally is that the flash pulse time is shorter than the time it takes the shutter to travel across the sensor. Therefore only a narrow band across of the subject shows as lit by the flash. **FP** works by firing a series of flash pulses in rapid succession.

Communication Light

The flash in the camera hot shoe which triggers the external flash also gives off flash light. If you want your external flash to be the main subject lighting this trigger flash can show up on the subject and interfere with the main light. You can minimize the effect of the trigger flash by reducing its power using the Communication Light setting. If set too low, the main light will not be triggered, of course. Many accessory flashes (Metz, for example)come with a cover for the hot shoe flash which blanks off the light while still allowing the trigger pulse through.

Wireless Setup

This is beyond the scope of my book and will be explained more fully in the manual of the wireless flash itself. Basically, you can control the firing method and relative power of the inbuilt flash and up to three external units from here. With 3 external flashes you could have a full power key light, half power fill in and quarter power background, say. You have individual choice of the mode of operation of each flash or switching it off altogether. Personally, I would set the Firing Mode to Manual and set each flash myself, doing test shots until I nailed the exact result I wanted. It would take time but such a setup could be used over and over again to give reliable multi-flash studio style lighting out in the field. Test by pressing the Disp button on the camera back or touching Test Flash on the monitor. Complicated but an invaluable facility to have. In reality, complex flash lamp setups are difficult to work with and most photographers will find it easier and more reliable to use two or three studio lights on stands. With these, whether flash or LED you will have proper modeling lights built in so that you can judge your setup by eye.

Photo Menu - Others (Photo)1

Bracketing

Exposure Bracketing (Fig 33)

Where light conditions are difficult, for example on a sunny day with someone half in and half out of a shadow, it can be difficult to know the correct exposure. Do you expose for the dark area, making the light area too light or the light area making the dark area too dark. Or somewhere in between? The camera's auto exposure cannot make this decision for you and it will try to find an average. This is not always the best decision. At its simplest, with **Exposure Bracketing** the camera takes three frames one after another, frame 1 at what the auto-exposure thinks is the correct exposure, frame 2 at half that exposure and frame 3 at double that exposure. You decide which exposure you like best after viewing the three exposures.

More Settings

gives you access to three parameters for **Exposure Bracketing**.

Step

Set to 7-1 it takes 7 frames one stop apart giving you a range from 3 stops under to 3 stops over exposure. 7-2 spans from 2 stops under to 2 stops over. 5 and 3 Step pro rata. You can see all this on the excellent graphic at the bottom of the setting Screen. I find **Step 3-1** the most useful. The S1's meter is rarely far off optimum exposure and if it is, frames 1 stop under and 1 stop over are usually enough.

Sequence

Gives you a choice of the order of bracketing. Since taking three shots takes longer than taking one, you may prefer to have the standard frame taken first just in case the subject moves. Or you may prefer the logical order from under to over=exposed.

Single Shot Setting

lets you set a burst mode so that instead of having to press the shutter button for each exposure, you can just hold the button down and they will be fired off sequentially until done.

Aperture Bracketing (Fig 34)

this will vary your aperture either side of your chosen setting. Set to f/5.6 and an **Image Count** of 3, it will give you shots at f/5.6, then f/4 and then f/2.8. Set **Image Count** to 5 and f/5.6 it will give you f/5.6, f/4, f/8, f/2.8, f/11. Set to **All** it will fire off shots using every **Aperture Setting** available from the widest to the smallest. Note that this will **not** alter your exposure which will remain constant. It will alter your depth of field, how much of your picture will be in focus or how blurred your background will be. Take care with this facility because while your shutter speed might be perfectly manageable at f/4, at f/22 the camera may have to set a slow shutter speed that is not easily handheld, 5 Axis Stabilization or not!

FOCUS

This takes a series of frames with the focus point shifted each time. For any given subject it is difficult to predict what steps and how many you will needs so you'll probably end up finding the best result by trial and error. **Step** sets the amount by which focus will be shifted in each shoot. This takes into account how far the subject is from the camera. The nearer the camera, the shorter the distance between the focus points since depth of field is more restricted the closer the subject is to the camera. **Image Count** is simply the number of images you wish to shot. You can take up to 999 but I doubt there are many subjects that would require over 100. **Sequence** determines the order of shooting the sequence. **0/+** Starts at the point where you have focused the lens and focuses progressively further away. **0/-/+** takes one at your focus point, then one closer and one further away until your **Image Count** is fulfilled. **Note:** These focus bracketed frames can be used for **focus stacking**, a technique widely used to extend depth of field for photographs of small objects, insects etc. It entails combining the focus bracketed images into one image exhibiting great depth of field which would be unobtainable with a conventionally taken macro shot, even with the lens stopped down. Most photo editing programs will perform the stacking.

White Balance Bracket(Fig 35)

this is redundant in **RAW** since you set the **White Balance** to your own taste in software afterwards. **More Settings** lets you **Bracket** A-B or M-G. A-B shoots one normal, one warmer, one cooler frame. M-G (Magenta/ Green) varies the tint of the image. The setting is necessary because whereas the eye (the brain, actually) compensates for lighting conditions in the real world, when it looks at an image it just sees what is there. Thus, on a clear day at midday natural light is quite blue. In the evening it becomes redder. Because the brain knows this from experience, it applies a correction so that a red object looks the same tone at midday or at 8 in the evening. The camera, however, can't do that and pictures taken at midday look bluer (cooler) than pictures taken in redder (warmer) late evening. **Auto White Balance** is the camera's answer to the brain's inability to automatically compensate for over cool or warm images in a photograph. It is (occasionally) fooled and Bracketing is designed to let you choose the best alternative. A-B bracketing is useful in daylight, M-G more so in artificial light from fluorescent tubes for example.

Color Temperature Bracket (Fig 36)

Not applicable in **RAW**. This brackets colour temperature in explicit terms of Degrees **K**elvin which is a scientific measure with absolute zero at -273K. Applied to photography, light from a candle will be around 2000K, very warm. In the shade on a day with a clear blue sky at noon, you'd have 8-10000k. This item does the same job as A-B (above) but lets you explicitly set the colour temperature in degrees Kelvin yourself. If I was unsure what colour temperature I wanted to set, I'd be inclined to shoot **RAW** which would enable me to choose any temperature I wanted in post processing.

<u>Silent Mode</u>

This could have been called stealth mode! It switches to the **Electronic Shutter**, turns off any shutter sound set, switches off the flash and system beeps etc. The only sound is the soft rustle of the aperture blades. It can be set to a **Fn** button and can

be memorized in **Custom** modes. A very handy
function for any situation where photography might
be considered obtrusive or a lightly sleeping baby
might be woken up!

Image Stabilizer

Operation Mode

• **Normal (Fig 37)**The image is stabilized in every
plane. This is the most effective for all uses except
panning.

• **Auto (Fig 38)** mode is designed for panning shots,
where you sweep the camera left/right or right/left and
more rarely up/down or down/up to keep a moving
subject in a fixed position in the finder while blurring
the background. The **Standard** mode is best for
normal use because it will operate the **Dual IS**,
combined lens and body stabilization which **Auto** will
not. However, **Normal** mode if used when panning
will interpret the blurred background as unwanted
camera movement and try to correct for it.

• **Note:** At shutter speeds over about 1/1000th it is as
well to switch off stabilization altogether. There is
little danger of camera shake at such a speed even with
a 300mm lens and the stabilization uses battery and
processing power. If you are shooting a sequence, that
processing power is better used tracking the subject.
The Auto setting only appears with native lenses. With
others you will see settings to enable horizontal or
up/down panning manually. When using Panasonic
lenses with their own stabilization, it is combined with
the body stabilization to give an enhanced stabilization
utilizing both, **Dual Stabilization**. For other makes of
lenses even those that have stabilization, it is best to
use the S1's own body stabilization

When To Activate

As previously mentioned, stabilization consumes battery power. Thus, it can be useful to only bring it to bear when it is needed. The **Half-Shutter** option does that, stabilization comes in on the half press and goes off upon release. The downside is that it takes the S1 a moment to sense the movement and start correcting for it. If you press the shutter button down fast for a quick shot of a fleeting subject, stabilization may not have had time to fully get a grip. **ALWAYS** does what it says, the camera corrects constantly so is always ready for a shot but at the cost of battery life. It's a hard call but I personally prefer to save the battery power. To be honest, I also enjoy the impression when I half press the shutter that a giant, steady, invisible hand has taken over the camera.

E-Stabilization (Video)

This adds extra stabilization on top of the normal for video only. It restricts the angle of view of the lens to give itself leeway to shift the image around on the sensor. I find the normal lens/body stabilization adequate for video but this is useful for use under extreme conditions, hand held walking shots, for example, where an unpleasant jittery or jarring motion can be smoothed out. Applicable in video only.

Boost I.S. (Video)

This is for video use only. It steadies the camera to the extent that sequences can look like they were shot on a tripod. It works less well with telephoto lenses. For it to work you must hold the camera in a fixed position. If you want to re-frame or zoom or move, you need to turn the **I.S.Lock** off while you do it. When it is in use, a hand icon will appear on screen to remind you not to move. Provided you accept the limitations, this is stunning facility to have for improving your video.

Focal Length Set

If you are using a non native Mount lens it will not have the correct contacts to set its focal length automatically. When you fit such a lens, the camera will ask you to set the focal length so that it knows what stabilization to apply. You can save 3 focal lengths in the box below the selector. To do this, select the focal length and then press the down arrow. Highlight the preset you want to replace, and press display. Confirm the dialog that appears and that focal length is now one of your presets.

Burst Shot 1 Setting

The S1 has an impressive array of Burst settings. **Burst I** and **II** let you pick your two most used settings and assign them here for immediate access. The **Burst** settings have become quite complicated with the S1. **Note:** 1. **Live View** means that the image in the EVF is where the subject is at the moment the frame is shot, in other words you are viewing in real time. When **Live View** is not possible, the image in the EVF is the frame just shot, so lags just behind real time. Some people find the lag disorientating, some don't. I do, so prefer the settings with **Live View** available. 2. When I say **MECH.** that includes using the **MECH>** with **Electronic Front Curtain**, **EFC** . 3. When set to a **Burst** mode, if you half press the shutter you will see a lower case 'r' appear on the bottom right of the

LCD Status panel or the monitor **Info Disp.**. The figure following is the maximum number of frames you can fire at the present **Burst** setting. **Note:** although the first choice always shows as **6K**, you actually have the option of **4K** as well for this setting. Go to **Rec→Others (Photo) 2→6K/4K PHOTO** to choose the burst type you want. Having done that, that will be the setting that **6K** represents.

• **6K** - See the note above. This uses the video autofocus routine, so don't expect it to keep up with a fast subject

• **H** - Using **AFC** or **MF** all shutter types give 9fps but no **Live View**. Using **AFC** as you generally would for a sequence burst, the **MECH.** shutter gives 6fps, the **E.** 5fps, both with **Live View**

• **M** - all shutter types give 5fps with **Live View**

• **L** - All shutter types give 2fps with **Live View**

 Notes

• I find **M**, giving 5fps the most reliable practical setting for most bursts. It is fast enough to capture the action and doesn't overload the S1's processor, leaving processor cyles free for keeping the focus accurate

• It reads exposure for each frame individually

• It gives a manageable number of frames for selection and editing

• I find it best for subjects like football or motor sport where your subject is moving fast and/or erratically. The higher frame rates, which restrict you to **AFS** or **MF**, are more suitable for a subject like a hurdler moving directly across your field of view. You can focus on the hurdle and shoot a high speed sequence as the athlete jumps and thus be sure of catching a good action moment

• For sport you will be shooting at a high shutter speed so won't need stabilization. Switch it off along with any other computer sapping functions like **Shading Comp.**

• Shooting **JPG** only, the S1 can keep a burst going indefinitely. If **RAW** is being shot, that reduces to around 90 frames and with **RAW+JPG** around 70 frames

• To get the best focusing results in a burst mode, make sure you have **Custom Menu→Focus/Shutter Priority→AFC** set to **FOCUS**

Burst Shot 2 Setting

Same choices as Burst Shot 1 Setting

Shutter Type

Any camera using a mechanical focal plane shutter (**MECH.**), effectively a blind with a narrow slit in it, which hurtles across the sensor at high speed will be subject to 'shutter shock' to some degree. It occurs, when it does, at shutter speeds between 1/60th and 1/400th (roughly) where the force of the shutter's first curtain hitting the frame edge causes a slight double imaging or blurring. To avoid this, the S1 has an electronic shutter (**ELEC.**) which has no moving parts and so cannot cause any shock. Unfortunately, the **ELEC.** has quirks of its own.

Auto

The S1 chooses the most appropriate shutter type depending on your current usage.

MECH.

The mechanical shutter. It can give speeds from 60 seconds to 1/8000th and can be used with flash.

56

EFC

A hybrid shutter action where the first operation is electronic and the second mechanical. It effectively eliminates any possibility of shutter shock, the disadvantage being that the top shutter speed is restricted to 1/2000th. It can be used with flash You could use this all the time but in strong light if you wish o use a wide apertures it is easy to find the top shutter speed a limitation.

ELEC.

A fully electronic shutter action. It can be totally silent or you can assign sounds to it (see later in this book) and it has a highest speed of 1/8000th. Why not use this all the time? Because you cannot use flash with it and any movement in your image can be prey to the 'jello' effect, a kind of sloping distortion due to the way the shutter operates. It uses less battery power but needs care under fluorescent light, where it can cause a banding effect. **Note:** There is a logic to using **Auto** all the time but I am never sure if or when camera will switch to **ELEC.** and potentially spoil pictures with the jello effect.

ELEC.+NR

When a long exposure is made, random noise is introduced electronically. It is a fact of life with any image sensor. This deals with it by making a second, blank exposure after your main one, seeing where the noise is and subtracting it from your image. The downside to this is that if you take a 10 second exposure, you must wait another 10 or so seconds before you can view it. Well worth it for the IQ improvement and I'd always use it.

Shutter Delay

This is useful for letting the camera settle down after the shutter button has been pushed. It can be used instead of a cable or remote release on a tripod but is also surprisingly useful for long hand held exposures, enabling you to remove your finger from the shutter release and settle the camera tightly against your body with both hands before it fires. I find a couple of seconds enough generally. **Note:** on pressing the shutter with **Shutter Delay** engaged, the monitor/EVF black out, coming on again after the exposure. The **Self Timer** does a similar job in delaying the firing of the shutter but the screen stays on during the delay time. **Self Timer** is intended for giving you time to get in a shot yourself and has no shake reducing effect.

Ex. Tele Conv.

This gives the effect increasing the apparent focal length of your lens without loss of image quality but only in the **M** and **S** image sizes. It amounts to little more than cropping the image and you might as well shoot as normal and crop later. For video, a telephoto effect without loss of image quality can be obtained using **Image Area of Video** setting in the **Video** menu.

Photo Menu - Others (Photo) 2

Time Lapse/ Animation

Mode

This sets **Time Lapse Shot** or **Stop Motion Animation**. The difference in operation is that **Time Lapse Shot** fires off the chosen number of frames at the chosen interval and then stops whereas **Stop Motion Animation** can fire at a chosen interval or manually and overlays the last two frames taken so that you can visually judge how far to move your subject for each consecutive frame. Both methods are compiled into a movie after shooting. **Note:** I'd suggest using the **ELEC.** for these operations to conserve battery power and prolong shutter life. With a projected life of 400,000 operations, at 30fps that equates to less than 4 hours of movie!.

Time Lapse Shot

This gives you those stunning effects seen so often on TV documentaries, where the sun moves across the sky or a building in 20 seconds or rush hour crowds zoom past the camera as if on wheels.

Shooting Interval Setting

How often the shutter should fire.

Start Time

Once you have set the parameters below either press **Now** and then the shutter button for an immediate start or **Start Time Set** to set the time you want it to commence. Let's say you wanted to make a **Time Lapse** sequence of the moon rising and setting over your house. You could set the **Start Time** to commence shooting in 8 hours and the **Shooting Interval** to 10 seconds with an **Image Count** of

2160. That would give **Time Lapse** movie of 2160 frames which at at 30fps would give you a video duration of 1m and 12s.

Image Count

How many images it should take before stopping. **Note:** To interrupt or stop the operation prematurely press **Fn1**. **Note:** at the bottom of the setting screen there is information to tell you what time and date your sequence will finish.

Shooting Interval

If you have set the camera to **Auto Shooting On**, choose how long to pause between frames while you adjust as necessary. **Note:** For complicated movements where you are making the adjustments and firing the camera yourself, it saves time to put the camera on a tripod and operate it remotely with your phone. Then you can sit near your move object just just out of shot, move it and fire off the shot immediately.

Exposure Leveling

Unless you are using artificial lighting, exposure can change between shots during your **Time Lapse**. This attempts to iron out any differences.

Stop Motion Animation

Do you want to make a pudding crawl? A teddy bear do the tango? This menu item makes it as easy as it can be. **Stop Motion Animation** is akin to **Time Lapse** but as I said previously after each frame it shows the last two frames overlaid, so you can judge easily how much you want to move your pudding or teddy bear.

Add To Picture Group

This will bring up previous **Stop Motion Animation** groups (that is, sets of **Stop Motion Animation** stills, not MP4s) stored on the SD Card so that you can add the new one on to them.

Auto Shooting

You can either have the camera fire the shutter automatically at set intervals or fire it manually yourself. If the movement to be carried out is repetitive and simple, just set the **Auto Shooting On** and move the object of movement incrementally with reference to the overlays. If the movement is more complex, set this **Off** and fire the shutter by hand.

Shooting Interval

If you have **Auto Shooting** on, how often do you want to shoot a frame?

Self Timer

delays the firing of the shutter for the specified time.

10 Seconds (Fig 39)

gives you time to get in the picture yourself.

10 second Multi-Shot (Fig 40)

delay and then takes 3 pictures at about 2 second intervals. If you are taken by surprise by the first shutter click, you have two more in which to compose yourself.

2 Second (Fig 41)

This is useful for letting the camera settle down after the shutter button has been pushed. It can be used instead of a cable or remote release on a tripod but is also surprisingly useful for long hand held exposures, enabling you to remove your finger from the shutter release and settle the camera tightly against your body with both hands. See also the **Shutter Delay** setting in the **Rec** menu which is similar but tailored to firing the shutter with the least possible shock.

Flicker Decrease (Photo)

Occasionally, usually under fluorescent lighting, the S1's EVF/Monitor may exhibit an unpleasant flickering effect. This attempts to decrease it. The flickering, when it occurs, is caused by the pulsating nature of some lamps and the scan rate of the EVF/Monitor. **Note:** this only operates with the **Mech.** or **EFC** shutter mode.

6K/4K PHOTO

To use this you must set the **Drive Mode Dial** to **Burst Shot 1 or 2 (Fig 42)** having assigned **6K/4K Photo** to one of them . To realize the highest possible speeds you will also need a fast UHS Class 3 SD card. These are the ones with a double row of contacts. They are backward compatible with older SD Card readers. **Note:** the Aspect Ratios available are **4:3** and **3:2**. Because these high speed modes use the electronic shutter (**ELEC.**) images may be subject to a movement distortion commonly called the jello effect. Focusing is automatically set to **Continuous**, the only other option being **Manual. Note:** The continuous focusing here is slower than **AFC** because the files being **MP4**, it uses the video focusing.

Picture Size / Burst Speed

The choices here are straightforward. **6K** offers a 4992px wide image at 30fps. **4K** offers a faster 60fps for a 3328px wide image or a slightly bigger one at 30fps using a 16:9 ratio. main reason to use **4K** over **6K** is the faster burst, of course. The sequence is recorded as an **MP4** movie file. You can extract the files you want to keep by pressing the **Playback** button and viewing the file. If you don't see it, a touch on the monitor will bring it up a **Select icon (Fig 43)**. Touch it and a series of controls comes up, enabling you to scroll through the frames, pin them for later retrieval and extract and save them by touching this **Save icon (Fig 44)**. When you do so, a confirmation dialog appears. At the bottom of the screen you will see **DISP.Reduce Rolling Shutter**. Touching this will have the S1 try to correct any of the rolling shutter (jello) distortion inherent when using the **ELEC.**. It will often say that it cannot correct this image but even if it does accept the image, its results are unpredictable, I find.

Rec Method

• **6K/4K Burst (Fig 45)** The burst will start when you press the shutter button and finish when you release it

• **Start/Stop Burst (Fig 46)** Press the shutter button to start the sequence which will continue until you press the button again

• **Pre-Burst (Fig 47)** The shutter button acts as if you are shooting a single shot so press it at the moment you want to capture. However, the S1 will record 1 seconds worth of the action from before you press the button to 1 seconds worth after, at your chosen frame rate. This sounds like a miracle but what it actually does is record constantly from when it is set. Then when you press the button, it saves the frames from before and after pressing. It is a great way of shooting something that happens very fast and suddenly, such as a bird landing on its nest. You can do the same thing with the other 2 **6K/4K** burst settings but you then have hundreds of frames to go through to find the right one. With **Pre-Burst** all the frames are relevant and you just have to pick the best

Pre-Burst Recording

This isn't available in **Pre-Burst** (above) which performs this function as part of its routine. With **Burst** and **Burst(S/S)** this gives you the images from 1 second before you press the shutter button. Again, it works by setting the camera recording from the moment it is set. Both this and **Pre-Burst** drain the battery quite quickly because the camera is recording all the time, so they shouldn't be used to simply shoot everything and pick afterwards. Besides, given potentially thousands of frames to from which to select, you will suffer from editing fatigue and quite likely miss the best shots! Panasonic warn that the camera may overheat if the pre-burst **6K/4K** modes are used excessively. So don't forget to turn the **Drive Mode Dial** to a normal shooting mode as soon as you are finished.

Post Focus

This gives you a choice of 6K or 4K shooting. Whichever you choose, the S1 makes a series of exposures covering all the salient focus points in the frame. The camera will then process the image into an **mp4** file, after which in **Playback** you can touch

Post Focus Play Icon (Fig 48) and then any point on the screen and focus will move there (unless the point is too close for focus, of course). If you touch the **Peak** icon, it will toggle peaking on and off so that you check the focus. Having ascertained where you want focus to be, you can save that image as a **JPG** by pressing the **Select icon (Fig 43)**. You can do this for as many focus positions as you wish. The **Merge (Stack)icon (Fig 49)** top right allows you to do what is usually called **Focus Stacking**, though Panasonic prefer to call it **Merging**. This blends the **Post Focus** images in such a way that your image looks like one with great depth of field. You can either have the camera merge the frames automatically, **Auto Merging** or pick a focus range yourself, **Range Merging**. For this, touch the areas of the frame you want in focus and touch the icon bottom right. **Note:** if you save all the frames to **JPG**, most imaging software will have a routine stitch them together. The S1 does it very well, however. You will have seen **Focus Stacking** used most often for very close up head-shots of insects where even stopping the lens right down would not provide enough depth of field to get the creature's head all sharp. **Note: Post Focus** needs to be used with a tripod to get its best results.

Multiple Exposure

This enables you to fire the shutter up to 4 times on one frame, combining the exposures. After setting the options below, you must initiate the multiple exposure from **Start**, the top item on the menu before pressing the shutter button. After the first shot a **Next/ Retake/ Exit** Dialog pops up giving you some control over the sequence as it progresses. If you set **Overlay** to **Off** in **JPG** or **RAW** quality, the first shot you make after pressing **Start** is the exposure onto which the subsequent ones will be layered. **On** cannot be used in **JPG** quality! Set **On** in **RAW** and you must select the image on which the subsequent ones will be layered from one previously taken one on your **SD card**. When you press **Start**, you will be taken to the previous images to make your choice of starting image. **Note:** You can only choose a **RAW** image.

Auto Gain

For most uses, **Auto Gain** is best left on. With it off you will have to set the exposure of each shot yourself which will involve a lot of experimentation. On the other hand, it could, with care, produce a result exactly to your liking. Play with this facility to see if you find it useful. Lots of fun experimenting with this and you can get some unexpected results!

Video Menu - Image Quality 1

Exposure Mode

Similar to stills. The best auto-exposure mode is shutter priority (**S**) with the shutter speed set to (numerically) double the frame rate. I shoot at 25fps so use 1/50th. It gives a natural looking movement but on a bright day may be too slow a shutter speed to be usable due to overexposure. In that case, either use a higher shutter speed and the hell with it or - better - buy some Neutral Density filters.**M**anual is is the professional choice. It avoids any amateurish flickering as the camera changes the exposure but does mean that as you move the camera a scene can be badly exposed. I use **S** mostly. **A** and **P** are viable choices but will likely choose a high shutter speed in bright light which can give a rather choppy effect to video.

Photo Style

This gives you a series of preset colour values other than the standard neutral output. Each can be customized with regard to **Contrast**, **Sharpness**, **Noise Reduction** and **Saturation**. I find all the default 0 settings good for my purposes except for **Noise Reduction** which at 0 is too aggressive for my taste. I set it to -5 since I am willing to accept some noise in return for maintaining sharpness. **Note:** Settings here apply to both stills and video, so if you set **Cinelike D** while shooting a movie, don't forget to re-set the **Style** before shooting stills.

Standard

Plain vanilla neutral values and the pick for general use.

Vivid

This is self-explanatory though I'd have called it Lurid.

Natural

Gives pleasantly soft colours.

Flat

Lowish contrast with almost pastel colours, it can look rather stylish with the right subjects.

Landscape

Souped up blues and greens.

Portrait

Warms the skin tones.

Monochrome

Black and white! When this is set a new option appear on the right of the screen. It allows you to select red, green, yellow or orange filters. These are the classic filters used in film days with red being the most dramatic, yielding dark, almost black skies that enhance the dramatic effect of any clouds. You can also add grain effects.

L.Monochrome

This is a nice gutsy black and white, great for moody landscapes. Do try the filters with this one!

L.Monochrome D

This is an even more gutsy monochrome for those gritty urban landscapes.

Cinelike D

This is mainly used by video makers but you may like it for stills. It is flat in contrast and is intended to use as much of the dynamic range of the sensor as possible, retaining the maximum detail in the shadows and highlights. Then, for post processing you can tailor the image to your liking. For stills, if you are going to this much trouble, you might as well shoot **RAW** which retains everything the sensor records and offers you maximum flexibility on post processing.

Cinelike V

Like the previous entry, this is mainly for video use. It is intended to give film like images which to my eyes looks quite like **Standard** but with slightly denser colours, somewhere between **Standard** and **Vivid**.

Like709

Video again. If you understand this highly technical setting, you probably don't need this book! Rec 709 is a colour standard used for high definition broadcasting. It is identical to sRGB. High end cameras have a wider gamut, or colour range than that, so Like709 is is designed to retain the whole gamut of the S1 by compressing the brightest areas to fit the monitor. You can then colour manage it in post precessing to get the result you want on your monitor. There's always the problem that it will look different on other monitors unless they are colour managed but there is little you can do about that.

Knee

This lets you choose the brightness point at which highlight compression will start (Point)and the fierceness (Slope) of the compression.

V-Log

Note: this only appears with the paid for firmware upgrade. **V-Log** was previously only available on Panasonic's professional video cameras. Used as is it gives a flat, dull image rendering which has the advantage of extending dynamic range by around 2 stops. It is not designed to be used as is, however. In post processing the colour is is 'graded' to provide a result pleasing to the videographers eyes. This means that over a series of sequences shot under different lighting conditions, the S1 provides a standardized result using the sensor's maximum quality. The grading can then take place so that the overall look of a movie can be matched from sequence to sequence. If you wish to see colours more closely aligned to how they might finally look while shooting, you can use an **LUT** (Look Up Table) which can be set in **Custom→Monitor/Display 3→V-Log View Assist**

MY PHOT STYLE 1-4

Here you can set the S1 to record video to your own specification in terms of contrast, sharpness, noise reduction, saturation (the intensity of the colours) and hue, the colours themselves. So, for example, if **Vivid** was not vivid enough you up the contrast and saturation sliders and save that as the new **Vivid**. You need to experiment with these to see what you prefer. **Note:** if you record in **MP4 HEVC** (see the **Rec.File Format)** in the **Image Format** section,, the **Photo Style** is fixed at **Like2100(HLG)**. This is only appropriate if you have a suitable TV.

Metering Mode

As in Photo→Image Quality 1→Metering Mode

ISO Sensitivity(video)

Sets the **ISO** for video, it is set separately for stills. It sets the lowest and highest settings the S1 will use when set to **ISO Auto**.

Flicker Decrease(Video)

This allows you to fix the shutter speed if you see flicker or striping on your screen.

i.Dynamic Range

Under difficult conditions, bright sunny days with deep shadows, for example, the S1 will try to adjust the exposure and contrast for best results. Not available for any **HLG** settings

Vignetting Comp.

if your lens vignettes noticeably, this will increase the **ISO** sensitivity at the image edges/ corners to compensate. It can lead to extra noise in those areas. It doesn't work with **High Speed Video**.

Diffraction Compensation

When a lens is stopped down beyond f/11 or so, diffraction, a form of blurring takes place. It is an optical phenomenon, not a fault. **Diffraction Compensation** sharpens the image up again. This is more often needed in video than stills, since with the lower shutter speeds used in video, the lens is often stopped down more than it would be in stills. The best way to deal with this is to use Neutral Density filters to cut down the light intake. A side effect of **Diffraction Compensation** can be more noise in the corrected areas of the image. **Auto** is a good choice.

Video Menu - Image Quality 1

Filter Settings

See Photo Menu→Image Quality 2→Filter Settings

Auto Exposure in P/A/S/M

This applies when you want to shoot a video directly from a stills recording mode by pressing the red **Video Rec** button on the back of the S1. With this set to **Off**, when you press the red button, exposure for the video continues at the the stills setting. If you press it with this set **On**, the S1 will ignore your settings and set exposure automatically, in practise a **P**rogram mode. **Note:** if you are shooting stills in **iA** mode and press the red button, the S1 will continue to set the exposure automatically.

Creative Video Combined Set

Video shooting and stills can have very different requirements but by default some S1 settings apply to both stills and video when set. This item enables you to set some of those parameters separately. If you usually shoot in **A**perture Priority, you set the **Mode Dial** to **A** and then set the parameters as you wish. To pluck one out of the blue, let's say you always shoot stills with **+2 Exposure Comp.**, **White Balance**→Flash, **Photo Style**→**Vivid**, **Metering Mode**→**Spot** and **AF Mode**→**Pinpoint**. Now set the **Mode Dial** to **Creative Video** and choose your preferred video settings. Let's say **-0+ Exposure Comp.**, **White Balance**→**AWB**, **Photo Style**→**Natural**, **Metering Mode**→**Multi-Metering** and **AF Mode→225 Area**. From now on, if you set any of these settings to the **Stills Camera icon (Fig 50)**, when you switch from stills to video on the mode dial, you will have your stills settings in video as well. Set to the **Movie Camera icon (Fig 51)** and when you change from stills to video mode and vice-versa, your chosen settings will change too.

Video Menu - Image Format

Rec Quality

For stills photographers, video, with its wealth of acronyms and dense terminology can seem more like a black art than photography. Here is an explanation of the main terms used by the S1. **Note:** the choices here will be governed by the settings in **Rec File Format** later in this menu.

• **FHD - 1920x1080** is the standard at the moment with **4K - 3840x2160** up and coming. **4K** monitors are not yet common but shooting in **4K** would future proof your work at the cost of greatly increasing the storage space required. One advantage of shooting **4K** is that it gives you scope for cropping when your final output is going to be **FHD**

• **Image Sensor Output** - **60p**, **50p 25p**, **24p** simply means the number of frames shot for every second of video. **60p** and **30p** are for use in regions of the world where the TV standard is **NTSC**, primarily the Americas, north and south. **50p** and **25p** are **PAL** and mainly for Europe and parts of Asia. They differ because of the different electrical mains frequencies used, 60Hz as opposed to 50Hz, which can cause flickering. In practise, it doesn't really matter since modern screens will handle either.

• Frames **P**er **S**econd - in theory, the more frames shot per second, the smoother will be any movement in the video. However **30p** and **25p** are the accepted standards and that is what devices and software are designed to use. **60p** and **50p** will be played back as half speed slow motion unless you have a device or software which can adjust the frame rate. **24**fps is the cinema standard. Enthusiasts consider the motion it produces more 'filmic'

• **420/8bit/LongGOP** - this refers to the chroma sub key sampling, colour bit depth and compression method respectively. Luckily, all S1 **MP4** formats deliver this same method so we don't need to worry our heads about it

• **Mbps** - **M**ega **b**its **P**er **s**econd. This is the main arbiter of video quality, the higher the better. The S1 doesn't give you a choice of bit rates so it only varies according to the format. Of course, while **60p** has twice the bit rate of **30p**, it doesn't imply better quality but simply reflects the fact that it is writing twice as much data per second

High Speed Video

Slow motion! One of the most used and enjoyed video effects ever. Only available in **Creative Video** mode. You need a fast SD card for this. Options from 1/6th speed to half speed. You cannot record sound with and focusing is automatically set to manual no matter what your normal video setting.

Rec File Format

For most photographers **MP4** will the best choice.

AVCHD

This was originally a format for Panasonic and Sony camcorders. It is intended for playback on TVs and Blu-Ray and offers no advantage over **MP4** It cannot shoot in **4K** and has no high quality options. It is also less convenient for use in video editing software.

MP4

This has become a de facto standard. It is the native format for YouTube and I use it for my YouTube Channel. It can be played back on just about every device and is easily edited, even on a mobile phone. If you want to shoot in **4K** you must use **MP4** since **AVCHD** cannot handle it.

MP4 HEVC

This is only available if the **Mode** Dial is set to **Creative Movie**. This retains image quality while yielding a smaller file. When set, **4K** is the only option available in **Rec Quality**. While you can view the video produced on the camera, it can only be viewed on a TV with **HEVC/H.265** support.

MOV

Note: This is only available with the paid firmware upgrade. A full range of **Rec Quality** settings is available for **MOV**. It is good for editing because it records 10 bit as opposed to 8 bit depth. 10bit records over 1 billion colours compared to 'only' 256 million for 8 bit so obviously gives more scope for post processing. 10 bit can only be used for editing since normal display media cannot use it. File sizes are bigger so a powerful computer is needed for editing.

Luminance Level

This is a highly specialist video setting. It doesn't alter your recorded image in any way, only the way it will be treated by post processing software. If you are going to be extracting stills from your video, **0-255** is best, as programs like Photoshop are suited to it. Otherwise, the default is **16-255**, it works perfectly well for extracting stills in practise and I can see no reason to change it.

Video Menu - Focus

AF Custom Setting(Video)

Video focus requirements are different from stills and to avoid unsightly and unsettling focus hunting issues **MF** is often best. If focus position is being changed during a shot, however, autofocus becomes necessary. To use Panasonic's best compromise, leave this setting **Off**. There will be occasions, though, where you find the S1's focusing not to your liking and you can tailor it here. **AF Speed** hastens or slows down how quickly the S1 transfers focus from the present position to a new one. **AF Sensitivity** controls how long the camera lingers on the present position before making the change. I find the settings are best set by doing a test shot and letting your instincts tell you how long to linger and how fast top change. A bit like the punch line to a joke, timing makes all the difference to the subjective effect of a focus change.

Continuous AF

Set to **On,** the camera continually focuses while recording. This setting overrides **S/C/MF** on the **Focus Mode** lever. You can make the camera readjust its focus setting at any time by half pressing the shutter button. Set **Continuous AF** to **Off** and the camera will focus when you start the video and not change unless you half press the shutter button. .**Note:** Most zoom lenses are not parfocal. That is to say, if you focus on a subject and then change the zoom length, it will not stay in focus. Some lenses do not go off focus as far as others but they will all go off focus. Refocusing combined with the zooming does not make for professional looking video so is better avoided or edited out in PP.

Focus Peaking

is a focusing aid that works with manual focus. It gives a graphic representation of which areas of your picture are sharply focused by highlighting the edges. It comes into its own in poor lighting when judging focus by eye is difficult but is also a useful tool for judging depth of field.

Focus Peaking Sensitivity

The lower the setting, the less prominent and the more precise the highlighting.

Display Color

Something that contrasts with the subject, usually. I tend to leave it set Red all the time, though.

Display while AFS

Peaking is normally used only in **MF** because that is when you need confirmation of your focus. In **AFS**, since the camera does the focusing - more accurately than eye, usually - you don't require confirmation. With this set **On** you will see the **Peaking** when you half press the shutter in **AFS**. It can be handy for confirming the focus point.

1-Area AF Moving Speed

If you are using **AF Modes→Face/Body/Eye/Animal Detect, 1-Area+** or **1-Area**, all of which display a single box focusing area, this sets the speed with which they respond to the Joystick or Cursor keys. Setting it **Fast** takes me back to Space Invader days

Video Menu - Audio

Sound Rec Level Display

This is only available if **Sound Rec Level Limiter** (below) is set **Off**. If sound levels are too high, a very nasty sounding distortion occurs. Displaying the **Sound Rec Level icon (Fig 52)** lets you monitor any overload. As a rule of thumb, the meter should only momentarily flash red on the very loudest peak sounds. I set it to peak just short of red for safety's sake since it is impossible to remove distortion but practical to increase volume in audio software. In some respects, getting good audio is a more exacting task than good video.

Sound Rec Level Adjust

Adjust the recording level for loud or soft sounds. You have from -12dB to +6dB. As a rule of thumb, start at -6dB and adjust up or down until the red light in the next to last box doesn't quite illuminate at the loudest point of your recording. If you are recording a guitar, say, have the player play the loudest section of the song and set the level to where that doesn't quite hit the red boxes. Sound levels can only be found by the suck it and see method.

Sound Rec Level Limiter

If you have set **Sound Rec Level Adjust** too high, this will prevent or limit the sound distortion caused. It is better to get it right from the outset and this setting can lead to loss of sound quality. A good back stop where levels are unpredictable.

Wind Noise Canceller

I leave this **OFF** for indoor shoots and
STANDARD for outdoor shoots without hearing
any unwanted effects. The threshold at which to
switch from **STANDARD** to **HIGH** is hard to fix
but if I can hear wind noise in my ears, I switch.

Mic Socket

If you use an external microphone in preference to
the S1's built in one, it may or may not need external
power to work. This enables you to set accordingly.
Line is for an input from a sound mixer or similar
device. Take care to get these settings right as your
mic can malfunction if not.

Special Mic

If you have Panasonic's DMW-MS2 stereo shotgun
microphone, this will alter its recording
characteristics. **Stereo** records over a wide area.
Lens Auto is very useful in that it limits the
recording area to the angle of view of the lens.
Shotgun makes the mic directional while **S.Shotgun**
makes it highly directional. If you feel the need you
can set the angle Manually.

XLR Mic Adapter Setting

For high quality recording you may need to use an
XLR mic. In that case you need to buy Panasonic's
XLR adapter which fits to the S1's hotshoe. This
setting determines whether sound from the XLR mic
will be added to the video, **On** or from the S1's built
in mic (**Off**)**Note:** if you have the paid firmware
upgrade, you have the option to use Hi-Res sound if
you are shooting in **MOV** file format.

<u>Sound Output</u>

If you monitor your audio through headphones you have two methods of listening. **REALTIME** lets you listen to the actual sound as it occurs. It won't necessarily reflect what is being recorded. **REC SOUND** lets you listen to the sound as it will be recorded. If there is overload distortion, you will hear it using this method. Unfortunately, it may lag the live sound you are hearing. Volume can be adjusted via the **Control Dial**

Video Menu - Monitor / Display

Waveform Monitor

Note: This comes with the paid firmware upgrade only. The **Waveform Monitor** has something in common with the **Histogram** but whereas the the **Histogram** tells you pixel brightness distribution in the image as a whole, the **Waveform Monitor** gives you the distribution as it is when viewing the scene. Thus if the image has a white poster on the left, the **Waveform Monitor** will show a peak on the left. The **Histogram** will add any other white pixels in the image to the ones forming the poster and show them as a total on the right. In other words, the **Waveform Monitor** is an abstract of the image itself shown in pixel brightness rather than pictorially. It's a handy tool but needs some study and experience to use it effectively.

HDMI Rec Output

If you are using an external **HDMI** screen to monitor your video recording, this determines whether shooting information will be displayed on the screen or not. If you are recording via the monitor, you will be wanting clean output and so set this to **Off**

Video Menu - Others(Video)

Image Stabilizer

When using **Creative Video** mode, only the video relevant settings are shown.

E-Stabilization(Video)

This works by cropping the image on the sensor a little, leaving a band of unseen pixels all around the image. The visible part of the image can then be moved around to compensate for movement of the camera. It s particularly well suited to correcting jittery camera movement of the type you get when shooting while walking. Since it crops in on the sensor, the angle of view for any given lens is narrowed a little. **Note:** If you are shooting for **FHD** output, shooting in **4K** gives you enormous scope for correcting camera movement in PP.

Boost I.S. (Video)

steadies the camera to the extent that sequences can look like they were shot on a tripod. It works less well with telephoto lenses. For it to work you must hold the camera in a fixed position. If you want to re-frame or zoom or move, you need to turn the **Boost I.S. (Video)** off while you do it. When it is in use, a hand icon will appear on screen to remind you not to move. Provided you accept the limitations, this is stunning facility to have for improving your video.

Image Area of Video

This is a way of giving a telephoto effect by narrowing the angle of view of any lens without image quality loss. A free telephoto lens! It works because the S1's sensor has an array of pixels big enough for stills picture definition, 6000x4000 pixels. Today's video, even **4K** at 3840x2160 , uses only a portion of that, **FHD** only 1920x1080. Normally, the S1 will use the full sensor area for video and then downsample it to the correct size. Using the **APS-C** area of the sensor, 3984x2656, the angle of view is narrowed a little. By using **Pixel/Pixel**, you get a narrower still angle of view. This uses the exact number of pixels of the video image size but works with **FHD**, 1920x1080 only. **Note: Pixel/Pixel** doesn't work with **High Speed** or **4k** video.

Custom Menu - Image Quality

Photo Style Settings

Show/Hide Photo Style

The **Photo Style**s menu contains many options and it is unlikely you will use them all. To avoid wading through them all to find your favourites, you can set the unwanted ones not to be displayed in the menu.

My Photo Style Settings

• **Add Effects** - this adds **ISO** and **WB** adjustments to the adjustments listed below your **My Photo Style**. It does not add them to the regular in built **Style** setting. This might be useful if you make a radical **Highlight** adjustment to your **My Photo Style** which darkens the image. You could up the **ISO** to compensate

• **Load Preset Setting** - this applies when you are using a saved **My Photo Style**, not the built in ones. Let's say in your Style you have all the adjustments at **+5**. You want, temporarily, to change the **Contrast** setting to **-5** setting. You do so and press **Set**. **Load Preset Settings** determines how how long your alteration will apply for before it is reset to your chosen setting of **Contrast +5** If **Change Photo Style** is set **On**, when you change to another style, your **Contrast** setting change will revert to its original **+5**. You can also have it change back the camera goes into **Sleep** mode or you turn the power off.

Reset Photo Style

This takes the **Photo Style** menu back to its default state, resetting all your **My Photo Style** Settings and any tweaks you have made to the built in settings.

ISO Increments

Set to **1EV**, when you press the **ISO** button on the camera and alter the values with the rear dial, the **ISO** values can be set to 100-200-400 etc. Set to values can be set to 100-125-160-200-250-320-400 etc, giving a more subtle choice of speeds at the expense of more dial twiddling. The smaller increments can be handy for video, where you will be working with a fixed shutter speed and so are more restricted in exposure options.

Extended ISO

Set to **Off** the lowest **ISO** you can set is 100 and the highest 51200. Set to **On** you can set from 50 - 204800. There is no IQ advantage to the settings below 100 and in fact a slight loss in dynamic range. The main use for this is on a bright day when you wish to use a wide aperture on your lens to limit depth of field and isolate your subject. With the 1/8,000th shutter speed available **Extended ISO** is not often necessary. Even on a very bright day with an exposure of 1/500th @ f/8 at 100ISO, a shutter speed with the S1's mechanical Shutter maximum 1/8000th will enable you to set the lens to f/2.

Exposure Offset Adjust.

If you find that your S1 consistently gives results too dark or too light for your taste, you can set an offset here for each **Metering Mode**. The adjustment stays in force until you change it. It differs from **Exposure Compensation** which is a temporary change for temporary circumstances. **Note:** if you set an **Exposure Offset Adjustment** of **+1/6 EV**, say, any **Exposure Compensation** applied to compensate for backlighting, say, will be added to the Offset. I would be wary of applying this adjustment to **Spot** mode, since **Spot** is very sensitive to small changes of position and not really stable enough in its readings to be universally offset. Remember, exposure is a creative control and lightness and darkness, within reason, are matters of taste, not correct or incorrect.

Color Space

• **sRGB** - This is a world-wide standard for colour space and is tailored to and best for digital images, general printing and Internet use. It is as close as you will get to ensuring that anyone looking at your image will see it as you did. That's not very close, since displays differ so much but it's the best we can do

• **Adobe RGB**

  This is more specialized and mainly for professional use. If you are working for the photographic industry, they will likely prefer images supplied in this **Color Space** since it has a wider **gamut**. A specialized professional (and expensive) monitor is needed. Without such a monitor, colours will be dull. It does not increase the range of colours the camera records (the gamut), only how they are interpreted by the display. **Note:** even if you shoot and edit in **Adobe RGB**, for general use you will export to **sRGB**. If you shoot **RAW** the **Color Space** is irrelevant, **RAW** being simply the binary data output from the sensor. Having edited your **RAW** image file you can export to any **Color space** required.

Exposure Comp Reset

  Set to **On**, any **Exposure Compensation** you have set will be reset to 0 if the camera recording mode is changed, from **A** to **M**, say or from stills to video and vice-versa. It is also reset to 0 if the S1 is switched off. I recommend leaving this setting **On**. It is very easy to forget you have an **Exposure Compensation** set when you switch off the camera and when you start the camera up again on an entirely different subject, wonder why it is over or underexposed. **Note:** The S1 has a good dynamic range and if you shoot **RAW**, you have an entirely usable couple of stops exposure leeway either way. This means that exposure can be tweaked to your exact taste in post processing. If you find yourself almost always adjusting exposure using **Exposure Compensation** you might want to consider **Exposure Offset Adjust.** which can apply compensation on a permanent basis.

Custom Menu - Focus Shutter 1

Focus/Shutter Priority

Which is more important to you? That you can always take a picture, even if it might be fuzzy? Or do you feel it isn't worth taking if it is going to be out of focus? Here's where you express your priority.

AFS

FOCUS If the picture will be out of focus, the camera will not release the shutter

BALANCE

Juggles the taking of pictures between focusing and release timing. This works well. If the picture would be slightly out of focus, the S1 will delay the shutter fractionally until the subject is in focus.

RELEASE

The camera will take the picture regardless of whether it will be in focus or not.

AFC

The choices same as above but for **AFC** so that it can be set separately. For sequence shooting **BALANCE** makes sense since **AFC** is less incisive than **AFS** and it would be a shame to miss a great sports shot because it was going to be slightly off focus.

Focus Switching for Vert / Horz

Doesn't operate when the **AF Area**, is set to **225-Area** or any of the **Custom** focus area modes. With this set **Off**, when you turn the camera from landscape to portrait orientation or vice-versa, the position of the **AF Area** stays put on the screen. With this **On**, wherever you last focused in either orientation is recalled.

AF/AE Lock Hold

This is only relevant if you have set a **Fn** button to
AFL/AEL. Set to **OFF**, when you press the **Fn**
button the **AF** and **AE** position/setting are frozen and
held only as long as you keep the button pushed. Set
ON, when you press the button the settings are
frozen and will stay that way until you press the
button again.

AF+MF

Normally, when you half press the shutter release,
focus is fixed all the while you hold it. With this **On**,
while the shutter is half pressed you can adjust focus
manually. This also works if you lock the focus via a
Fn button set to **AF/AE** or when the **AF ON** button
is pressed.

MF Assist

When manually focusing, it can be helpful to have
the magnify the portion of the scene on which you
wish to focus.
• **Focus Ring -** the screen will enlarge each time you
turn the focusing ring
• **AF Mode/MF (Fig 53)** - the screen is enlarged when
you press the **AF Mode Button (Fig 53)**
• **Joystick** - the screen is enlarged when you press the
joystick
• **MF Assist Display** - sets how the enlarged portion is
displayed. Either **FULL** which fills the screen with the
enlarged portion or **PIP** which opens a moveable
window within the display. You can alter the image
magnification with the front and rear dials

MF Guide

Because most modern lenses do not have stops at infinity and closest focus, it can be difficult to be sure when you are at either point. With **MF Guide** set **On** the **MF Guide (Fig 54)** comes up on screen when you turn the **MF** ring You can set the guide to metres or feet.

Focus Ring Lock

Disables the focus ring. There are many occasions, macro work among them, where manual focus is the easiest way to establish focus precisely , especially since the S1 can magnify the focus area to aid you. It is then only too easy to jog or disturb the ring the ring just enough to lose the critical focus you have obtained. Having determined your focus, set this item **ON** and it will stay where it is.

Show/Hide MF Mode

If you find there are some **AF Modes** that you never use, you can hide them from the choices available when you press the **AF Mode button (Fig 53)**

Custom Menu - Focus Shutter 2

Pinpoint AF Setting

Pinpoint AF Time

If You have the **AF Mode** set to **Pinpoint (Fig 55)**, on half pressing the shutter release a magnified view of the focus area appears in the viewfinder for a set period before the viewfinder reverts to its normal view. This period can be Short, Mid, or Long. You can also set the magnified view to fill the screen or be displayed in a window, **PIP**.

Pinpoint AF Display

The magnified view can either appear **FULL** screen or a **PIP** (Picture In Picture) - in a window

AF-Point Scope Setting

This adds a layer of precision to the **AF Point** positioning. It will only work if you have a **Fn Button** set to **SCP AF-Point Scope**. By default it is set to **Fn1** on the front of the camera body. When you press **Fn1**, the centre of the image area is enlarged and the focus point is set temporarily to **1-Area** with a very small focusing box. When you half press the shutter the focus is set to that small area, giving great precision. You can control whether the entire screen is filled with the magnified area or whether it shows as a window in the centre of the area with **PIP Display**. **Keep Enlarged Display** controls whether the enlarged area shows only while you keep the **Fn** pressed or whether you press the button to invoke it and again to dismiss it. Very handy for hand held close up work, an insect in a flower, for example.

Shutter AF

Controls whether a half press of the shutter release causes the camera to focus.

On

When you press the shutter release half way, the camera will focus.

Off

The shutter release simply fires the shutter

Half-Press Shutter

Controls the action of the shutter release button.

Off

The shutter release has a two stage action, rather like the trigger of a gun. Press the release and there is a detente half way. Press a bit harder and the shutter fires. If you have **Shutter AF** set **ON** then **Half Press Release** gives you a definite 'switch' feeling for focusing at the detente.

On

The shutter fires in one smooth action. It has the feel of a hair trigger about it. Great for sports and action, it makes the camera feel very responsive. It can feel a bit uncertain where focusing is concerned.

Quick AF

ON

when your camera is being held steady it assumes you will take a picture and adjusts focus so that when you do press the shutter it should be a bit quicker. It's a bit haphazard because if you have the camera in your hand at your side it will focus on whatever is next to you. It can be an aid to fast target acquisition but as often as not it just gives the camera more focusing work to do.

Eye Sensor AF
ON

When you put your eye to the viewfinder the camera focuses without any need to half press the shutter button. Can save time.

Looped Focus Frame
Off

when you move the focus area box around the frame using the Joystick or Cursor buttons, it stops at the edge of the frame.

On

if the focus area box reaches the edge of the frame it reappears on the opposite side in one smooth movement.

AFC Start Point (225 Area)

This functions in **AFC** with the **225 Area** focusing mode. Normally in **225 Area** the S1 works out which part of the scene to focus on. If you set this item **On**, the **225 Area** grid icon is overlaid with the letters **AFC** and a dialog box AF Area is displayed. Press that and you can set the start area wherever you wish using the touch screen, Joystick or Cursor buttons. Handy if you have a subject entering the frame from the left side of the frame, say, so you can set the focusing to pick up the subject there and follow through, where otherwise it might focus on the background and take time to sort itself out.

Custom Menu - Operation 1

Q.Menu Settings

When you press the **Q Button (Fig 56)** the Quick Menu appears. This is a handy way to access items that, while not changed frequently enough to merit setting to a **Fn**, still need quick access.

• **Layout Style - Mode 1 shows you the menu with the live view in a window. Mode 2 uses the whole screen for the menu, no live view.**

• **Front Dial Assignment** - You can either scroll through the items with the front dial in which case you change values with the rear dial or change values with the front dial and scroll through items with the **Cursor** keys or Joystick

• **Items Customize (Photo)** - you can set 12 items to display in the **Quick Menu**. If you want to change a default, highlight it and press **Menu/Set**. From the two tabs that appear select the item you want and press **Menu/Set** again

• **Items Customize (Video) - as for Photo**

Touch Settings

Lots of useful settings here to do with the monitor here.

Touch Screen

Off, the touch screen does not function. You must operate the camera via buttons and dials. Given the superb screen sensitivity and functionality for menu operations, for example, you may not want to disable it entirely.

Touch Tab

On, the tabs for **Fn** Buttons 7 to 11 , touch screen exposure etc appear on the right side of the screen.
Off You have a clear and uncluttered screen.

Touch AF

AF

when you touch an area of the monitor the camera will focus there.

AF+AE

When you touch an area of the monitor the camera will both focus there and optimise the exposure for that spot..

Touch Pad AF

When your eye is to the viewfinder you can still set the **Focus Area** position by touching the (now blank) monitor screen. This was a a major aid on Panasonic cameras until the advent of the **Joystick**. Worth trying, though. You may prefer it.

EXACT

touch the screen and focus is set at that position.

OFFSET

touch the screen and drag focus to where you want it. I find **Offset** the more intuitive

OFF

Unfortunately, with **Touch Pad AF** enabled it is very easy to accidentally move the focus position with your nose. **Off** solves that problem or you can disable the **Touch Screen** with **Operation Lock Lever**.

Lock Lever Setting

There are some controls on the S1 that you may find you operate inadvertently. You may find that with your eye to the EVF, your nose touches the monitor and the **Touch AF** operates, moving the focus area box. Or the palm of your hand presses the cursor keys when you operate the **AF ON** button. **Lever Lock settings** lets you quickly individually disable the Cursor keys, Joystick, Touch Screen, Dial and Disp. button when the lever is set to its lock position.

Fn Button Set

This enables you to assign functions of your choice to the S1's physical and virtual (on the right side of the monitor) **Fn** Buttons. Given the Quick Menu, My Menu, the **Fn** buttons and all the dials and wheels the S1 is customizable to a bewildering degree. Each button has around 75 assignable functions available! The defaults are pretty sensible and a good starting point. The only suggestion I have - and what I do myself - is to note what functions I use most over time and set them piecemeal to the **Fn** buttons. Apart from this menu setting, if you press and hold any **Fn** button it will bring up its present setting and enable you to change it. You can also bring up the settings with a press on the Fn icon on the monitor recording Info. screen. Not only are there a comprehensive array of buttons, there is a bewildering array of ways to access them too! Oh yes, and they can be set separately for Recording Modes and Playback Mode. Not only that, button assignments are saved with Custom Settings and Save/Restore Camera Settings so you can assign **Fn1** to Shutter Type in C1 and Peaking in C2 and so on! It's a good reason to back up your settings in Save/Restore Camera Setting. **Note:** if you want to use the Joystick as **Fn8-Fn12** you will need to expressly enable it in **Custom→Operation 2→Joystick Settings**. You will also find a setting in here which is unavailable elsewhere in the menu system, the **AF-ON** button now allows you to select normal operation or with a **Near** or **Far Shift**. Sometimes the focusing in the **225-Area** mode has a tendency to default to the background. Near bias will minimize that tendency, so is useful for situations where you want focus to be on a relatively small subject against a far background. **Far Shift** will, naturally, bias the focus towards distant rather than near subjects. Thus it will not attempt to focus on a cyclist approaching the camera when you are making a landscape picture. The simple **AF-ON** setting will make an intelligent assessment of your wishes balancing near and far subjects. When set to a **Near** or **Far Shift**, the bias only operates on focusing with the **AF-ON** button. With normal focusing via a half press of the shutter no **Near/Far Shift** is applied.

Fn Lever Setting

This is the small lever on the front of the S1. It is good for strategic change to the S1's operation because it is easily remembered and can be done by feel while the camera is held to your eye. I use it to switch between the **MECH.** and **ELEC.** shutters.

WB/ISO/Expo. Button

This sets how the **WB/ISO/Exposure Compensation** buttons on the top of the camera grip operate.

• **While Pressing** - press and hold down the button while you change the value using the Joystick or dials. Let go and it is set

• **After Pressing>** - press and let go the button.
Change the value. Let go the button
• **After Pressing** - a neat one, this. Each time you press
the button, it increments the setting upwards. When it
reaches the maximum value it loops back to the
minimum and starts again. **Note:** this setting doesn't
work with **Exposure Compensation** which simply
brings up the settings for you to alter with the usual
dials etc

ISO Displayed Setting

This sets the action of the front and rear dials when
the **ISO** button is pressed. You can have both dials
change the **ISO**, only the front or rear with the other
one inactive or one to change the **ISO** and one to set
the **ISO Limit** when you are using **Auto ISO**

Exposure Comp. Disp. Setting

• **Cursor Buttons (Up/Down)** - allows you to set
exposure **Bracketing** at the same time as **Exposure
Compensation**. You can set any flavour of
Bracketing using the Up/Down Cursor buttons while
operating the **Exposure Compensation** button
• **Front/Rear Dials** - allows you to configure the dials
to adjust flash exposure on the **Exposure
Compensation** screen

Custom Menu - Operation 2

Dial Set

this assigns roles to the front and rear dials in **P/A/S/ M** modes. **Set 1**, the default will be most photographers' choice. The **P** with diagonal arrow means the **P**rogram mode shift values. Whatever exposure **P** has set, when you turn the dial it will increment the aperture and shutter speed settings in a way that keep the exposure constant, opening the aperture as it speeds up the shutter and vice-versa.

Joystick Setting

While it can be disabled with **Off**, I don't think many will want to do that. The Joystick can be used to double up on the **Menu/Set** button functions or as **Fn** buttons 8-12. It is very fast and versatile as a **Fn** selector but its real functionality is brought out by **D.Focus**. In this mode it makes **Focus Area** control instinctive and responsive. Just move it up, down, left or right or diagonally to place the **Focus Area** to precisely where you want it. Any moment you want to centre the **AF Area**, just press the Joystick. Press it in again and **AF Area** toggles back to the previous focus position. While using the Joystick, the **Rear Dial** will alter the **Focus Box** size and you have **Focus Mode**, **AF Mode** (225 Area, Pinpoint etc) and **AF Area** position and size all within thumbs reach and - with a little familiarization - changeable without taking your eye from the **EVF**

Illuminated Button

Obviously handy for night time use, the button illuminates the **Playback**, **Q**, **Back**, **Delete** and **Disp.**

buttons. Most importantly, it light the **Status LCD** panel too. It doesn't illuminate itself! **Off** means the button lights the only. **On1** keeps the illumination on all the time the S1 is turned on. **On2** keeps the illumination on for 5 seconds then switches it off if the camera is idle. **Note:** the button does not illuminate itself!

Video Rec Button (Remote)

 If you have a shutter remote control you can use it to start and stop video recording. Set this menu item **Off** and the red dot **Video Rec** button is disabled to prevent accidental operation.

Custom Menu - Monitor / Display 1

Auto Review

If you like to check your image immediately after taking it, this sets the S1 to do so automatically.

Duration Time (photo)

This sets the **Auto Review** for still images only. The image can be held on screen from 1 to 5 seconds before reverting to the live view or, using **HOLD** until you touch the monitor or half press the shutter button. The image will be seen on the monitor or EVF depending on which you are using. Setting an **Auto Review** time does not freeze the camera for that period. If you press the shutter button the view will revert to live and your picture will be taken.

Duration Time (6K/4K PHOTO)

You obviously cannot **Auto Review** a burst of images but **HOLD** compiles the **6K/4K** output into a 'heap' so that you can step through them one by one. The number of the images in the sequence is shown at the top of the screen. **HOLD** is highly useful because usually you will shoot **6K/4K** bursts when you are not certain you will get a particular shot. Confirmation that you have or otherwise is key.

Duration Time (Post Focus)

As **6K/4k** but pertaining to **Post Focus** only.

Playback Operation Priority

sets what happens if you operate the controls while the recorded image is being **Auto Review**ed. Set **On** the buttons behave as if the camera was in **Playback** mode. So, press the **Left Cursor**, for example you will step back through previous images and you can delete the image immediately with the **Delete** button.

OFF, the controls behave as if the camera was in **Rec** mode and on pressing any of them the **Auto Review** screen will revert to live view and the button perform its normal **Rec** mode function.

Constant Preview

This takes effect only in manual (**M**) exposure mode. Normally in **M** mode, the S1 will keep the live view screen at a pretty constant brightness level. This is useful in something like a night shot of a dimly lit street so that you can see to compose your picture. On the other hand, **M**anual exposure is often used when the photographer wants to have explicit control over the exposure. If your night shot scene includes street lamps, your picture will look very different if exposed for the area lit by the lamp or for the shadow area in a doorway. If you set **Constant Preview** to **On**, as you open and close the aperture or raise and lower the shutter speed, the actual effect on the image will be seen. Whilst you wouldn't want that for everyday auto shooting where a bright and even live view aids fast composition, for **M**anual you would usually want to see the effect.

Set

Preview While MF Assist

this applies when **Custom→MF Assist→MF Assist** is **On**. Set **Preview While MF Assist** to **Off** and the manual focus assist box area will remain bright even though the screen may be dark. Set to **On**, the manual focus assist area will be as dark as the main scene area.

Level Gauge

This sets the **Level Gauge** to display or not. If you set it to **On** it displays permanently. While I use the gauge as a matter of course, I prefer to set it to display via **Fn** button since I prefer it only to be seen when I explicitly need it. The gauge shows you when the camera is level in both the horizontal and vertical planes, via a green line across the frame and two green dots in the centre for vertical.

Histogram

This controls whether you see the **Histogram (Fig 57)** when you cycle through the screens via the **DISP.** button on the camera back. A **Histogram** can be used as an exposure aid. It is a sort of graph of the pixels that comprise your image and how many of them there are at each level of brightness. The bottom of the histogram, the X axis, represents the brightness range of the image, with 0, black on the left and 255, white on the right. The Y, vertical axis, represents how many pixels of that tone there are in the image. A normal or average image will contain a range of tones from black to white with a majority in the mid range, so it will look like a hill in the **Histogram (Fig 58)** . If the peak is to the left, there is a preponderance of dark tones in your image, if right, a preponderance of light ones. This might be because your image is mainly composed of light or dark tones but generally it will indicate over or under exposure. Some **Exposure Compensation** will shift the peak towards the centre and balance your exposure for the subject in front of the lens. The **Histogram** is too sophisticated a tool to go into detail in a book like this. They are most useful when

used in the light of experience since real world
subjects don't conform to any simple rules!

Photo Grid Line

You can add **Guide Lines** to the display to aid
composition or subject placement. If set to the **Grid
icon (Fig 59)** you can move the lines around the
screen using the Cursor Buttons.

Framing Outline

This displays a thin, subtle light grey line around the
perimeter of the EVF and monitor. It can be useful in
Manual mode when **Constant Preview** is set **On**,
meaning the screen can go really dark of exposure is
low.

Center Marker

A cross is shown in the centre of the screen.
Convenient for re-aligning a scene which you are
shooting over the course of time or centering a zoom
- line up the marker with the subject's eye, say, keep
the marker on the eye and zoom in. One of those
little additions that is more use than you thought it
would be.

AF Area Display

In the zone based **AF Modes** (excepting **225-Area**)
this shows a permanent outline of the area within
which the S1 will focus. Useful with moving
subjects so that you can make sure the focus area is
kept on the subject. The smaller the focus zone the
quicker the S1 will find its focus since it has less
computation to do. The more accurately you can
place your moving subject in the focusing area the
less focus will stray from your subject.**Note:** this
doesn't operate with video and **6K/4K Photo** If you

amend a focus zone you must save it to a **Custom** mode for the S1 to recognize it..

Custom Menu - Monitor / Display 2

Live View Boost

 If you are photographing in a very low lit place and the monitor image is uncomfortably dim, this will boost it. The image will probably appear rather noisy but this won't be reflected in your recorded picture. This really only comes into its own in very, very dim conditions, under star light, for example. **Set** allows you to apply it to all exposure modes or restrict it to **M**anual only.**Mode 1** gives mild boost at some cost to the fluidity and quality of the EVF/Monitor quality. **Mode 2** gives a bigger boost in brightness but at great cost to viewing quality.

Monochrome Live View

 shows the monitor and EVF in black and white. It doesn't affect the image you record which will still be colour. Under some circumstances, manual focusing is facilitated by a mono view. Apparently.

Night Mode

 If you find the brightness of the **EVF** or **Monitor** is dazzling or affecting your perception of the scene you when photographing at night or in very dim surroundings, this applies a red tint reducing the contrast between view and reality. You can set the **EVF** or **Monitor** separately. Pressing Disp. allows you to adjust the brightness of the red screen. This mode is very effective for work like starlight photography where even a glimpse of a bright screen needs recovery time before full night vision is restored.

LVF/Monitor Disp. Set

This controls where the main shooting information is displayed on the EVF and Monitor respectively. You can either have the info displayed in a black bands outside of the scene or superimposed on the of the scene itself. Info is displayed in a black band outside of the viewing area. This setting gives a smaller image but keeps the view uncluttered. Info is displayed on scene itself. This setting maximizes the image area but the info is superimposed on the image itself which you may find distracting. Note: Though the S1's EVF is eminently viewable and the largest on any mirrorless camera, if you wear glasses and have difficulty seeing the full width of the screen, it is worth seeing if the smaller image setting can alleviate the problem. Note: this menu entry interacts with the **V.Mode** button on the right of the EVF housing. I find I get the best of all worlds by setting the info to display outside the view area with the V.Mode set to its largest view.

Expo.Meter

controls whether you see a graphic of an exposure meter when you turn the front or rear exposure dials. If you set it **ON** but don't see it when you change exposure parameters, press the **Disp.** button until it appears on the detailed information display. It lingers for a few second after changing settings. You have a numeric display of your current exposure on screen whether you have this on or not.

Focal Length

When you are using zoom lens, this displays the focal length setting of the lens for a few seconds after changing it.

Photo/Video Preview

Under normal shooting settings, angles of view for a given lens are much the same for stills or video, so if you are shooting stills and then press the **Video Rec.** button, you know what angle of view you will get. However, if you have set the **Video→Others→Image Area Of Video** to **APS-C** or **Pixel Pixel**, you will get a much narrow angle of view in video. This setting enables you to preview Still or Video settings so there are no surprises in store when you change.

Photos/Videos Remaining

The **EVF** and **Monitor** show a letter **r** followed by a number. The **Status LCD** shows just a number. The number can either be the amount of video shooting time left or the number of exposures remaining at your current quality setting. This item allows you to choose which.

Custom Menu - Monitor / Display 3

Show/Hide Monitor Layout

The S1's monitor steps though a series of screens when the **Disp.** button is pressed. One screen shows only the image with shutter Speed/Aperture and Exposure Compensation settings appearing when the shutter is half pressed. The next shows additional information such as Stabilization mode, White Balance, Image Quality and more. The next two are optional, a **Control Panel** screen and the screen turned off. This setting enables you to display or not the blank screen and the **Control Panel** screen. The **Control Panel** screen not only displays comprehensive information but any of the parameters shown can be altered using touch, the Joystick or the Cursor keys. It's a very flexible way of setting the camera. The blank screen is useful for saving battery power. **Note:** if you have the **Fn** buttons and **Quick Menu** well set up you may not need the **Control Panel**, especially with the major settings viewable at all times via the **Status LCD**. If you prefer, rather than disable the monitor via the blank screen, you can turn it off with the **LVF** button on the left of the EVF housing.

Blinking Highlights

With this **On** any overexposed areas will be shown blinking in black and white. It's an alternative to the more configurable **Zebra Pattern**, below and I go into more detail there.

Zebra Pattern

A pattern of diagonal lines indicates saturated highlight areas of your picture which will contain no detail. Over-exposed white areas in a picture or video look particularly unpleasant and harsh. The **Zebra Pattern** shows you where this problem is occurring (**Zebra1**) or about to (**Zebra2**)

Set

Allows you to set the zebras to occur at your chosen levels, from 50% to 105% in each case. The defaults of 100% (saturated) and 80% (close to saturation) are well chosen. The remedy to blown highlights is to apply minus exposure compensation. This is where the **Histogram** is useful. You try to adjust the exposure so that the hill-like shape in the Histogram graph does not exceed the borders. In some cases a scene will simply have more contrast than the camera can handle and the decision over what to do can be made only by your own eyes.

V-Log View Assist

If you are using **V-Log** in **Video→Photo Style→Image Quality 1**, this allows you to use **LUT**s (Look Up Tables) to view colours to your choice on monitor or via the **HDMI** output. This can be necessary since **V-Log** records a dull, flat picture designed for grading, that is setting colours to your choice, in PP. The technicalities of doing this are beyond the scope of this book.

HLG View Assist

Monitor

If you are shooting **Photo→Image Quality 1→HLG Photo** the S1 will display them on the screen looking very dull and colourless. That is because they are formulated for display on an **HLG** capable TV or external monitor. If you set this item to **Mode1** or **mode2**, images will be viewed and displayed in a natural looking form. **Mode1**converts with an emphasis on the reproduction of bright areas like the sky. **Mode2** emphasizes the reproduction for the main subject and will be the generally more useful one.

HDMI

this does the same as **Monitor** but with the **HDMI** device output. It has the addition of **Auto** which ascertains whether the device supports **HLG**. If it does, the conversion is left to the device. If it doesn't, **Mode2** conversion is applied.

Sheer Overlay

This could be of use to anyone who wants to record the same scene over a long period of time but cannot leave the camera in situ. Or, if doing product shots, matching an update to a previous offer. **Image Select** - find and select the image you want to use as the overlay. The overlaid image does not appear on the picture taken, that is to say, this does not do multiple exposure.

• **Transparency** - sets the transparency, the strength of the loaded image
• **Image Select** - choose the image you want to match or reference
• **Reset at Power Off** - cancel the overlay when you power off. Prevents confusion on startup!

I.S. Status Scope

If you are working under conditions where even the S1's stabilization is having problems keeping the image steady - on a boat, for example, this can come in handy. As far as I can work out, any movement of the green dot contained within the inner circle can be steadied fully. Within the outer circle shake can be contained adequately. Outside of that it is beyond stabilization. What you see on screen is the stabilized image with the dot dancing around to show you the work it is doing. Very useful with a very long lens because the Scope can help you find a hold or support that enables the stabilization to function adequately. Unless you want to frighten yourself, I suggest you don't use this after a night out!

Custom Menu - Lens / Others

Lens Focus Resume

Normally when you turn the camera off, the lens is reset to infinity focus. With this you can retain the focus setting when the S1 is turned off and on again.

Focus Ring Control

Most modern lenses are fly-by-wire, meaning there is no direct mechanical contact between the focusing ring and the lens assembly being moved to later focus distance. This control enables you to to set how the lens focusing responds to your input on the focusing ring. This applies to **M**anual focusing only, obviously.

• **NON-LINEAR** - the focusing responds to the speed with which you turn the ring. If you turn the ring quickly, less movement is required for a big focus change and the focusing can appear to bound through its range. Turn it slowly and the focusing becomes more measured.

• **LINEAR** - the focusing responds directly to how much you turn the ring

• **Set** - this lets you choose the angle through which the focusing ring must be turned to take the lens from infinity to nearest focus. It is most useful in **LINEAR** mode

Setup Menu - Card/File

Card Format

This deletes everything on the Card(s) and sets it up to work correctly with the S1. If you buy a new card it is as well to insert it to the camera and format it before use. If you have a problem with an card, **Format** is the first thing to try to correct it. It differs from **Delete All** in the Playback mode in that it will also delete any settings you have saved under **Save/ Restore Setting** as well as all files.

Double Card Slot Function

Recording Method
Relay Rec (Fig 60)

This treats the cards in the 2 slots as one big card. It records everything to one slot and when that is full continues to record seamlessly to the other.
Destination Card Slot sets which card should be recorded to first.

Backup rec (Fig 61)

This records to both slots simultaneously. Each card will contain the same material. It guards against the failure of a card.

Allocation Rec (Fig 62)

This treats each card as a separate entity. When selected, you are presented with a choice of destinations for the S1's shooting possibilities. If you use Lightroom, it is handy to set **JPG** and **RAW** to different cards as LR makes a bit of a mess of **RAW+JPG** imports. I use the JPGs for any immediate use while only importing the **RAW** files. This keep them nicely separate. **Note: Double Card Slot Function** isn't available if you shoot **AVCHD** format video as video cannot be recorded to **XQD** cards.

Folder / File Settings

In general the default file and folder naming of the S1 works well and there is little need to change it. The folders start at 100_PANA and each one will hold 999 image files. The 1000th image will cause a new folder to be created, 101PANA and so on. You could create a folder called MYFOL if you prefer. The prefix number will still increment so if if the camera was at 102PANA, your folder will be 103MYFOL. The R number on the right is the number of files the folder will accept. An empty folder may not show 999 files - that is because it starts from the last file number even if it has been deleted. Thus, if you shoot 400 images in 102_PANA and then delete them, the next image file number will be ****401 and the capacity will be R - presumably standing for Recording(?) - 599. You cannot reset the folder numbers to 100*****. They will increment to *****999 and then reset. You can reset the file numbering (see **No. Reset**). Image file names will always start with an _ (underscore) or a **P**. The underscore denotes an **Adobe RGB** colour space file, the **P** denotes a **sRGB** file. **Adobe RGB** has a wider colour gamut but should only be used for professional purposes where a client requests it. It does not enlarge the range of the sensor, merely writes more colours in the available range to give professional users more colours to play with. Used with normal display devices, it can give a flat, compressed appearance to images. The professional user will output **Adobe RGB** to **sRGB** for general use. **sRGB** is the de facto standard because it encompasses the colour range of modern monitors, TVs, smartphones etc.

Select Folder (SD1)

If you have created a folder in the **Slot 1**, this tells the S1 to save files to it.

Select Folder (SD2)

As for the previous entry but Slot 2, of course.

Create a new folder

You can create a new folder with the 5 letters/numbers of your choice here. **Create Folder** tells you the folder name protocol that will be used. Use change to redefine it.

File Name Setting

Lets you choose the file name protocol. If you were shooting for a client named Jim, you could change the name settings to PJIM**** for easy identification. **Folder Number Link** sets the S1 to use the 3 digit folder number as part of the file name, so if the folder is 103MYFOL, the image file names in that folder will be P103****.

File Number Reset

This works separately for each slot. It resets the File Numbers to start from *****001. It cannot start from the same folder, of course since it may have a previously shot image with that file name. So, it makes a new folder and starts from *****001. If the last image you shot was PS13020.jpg in folder 103MYFOL, after a **No.Reset** you will have a new folder, 104MYFOL and the first file in that will be PS14001.jpg. If you want to start everything from scratch, including the folder sequence, first of all

Format the card, then perform a **No. Reset**. If you say **Yes** to **Reset** File and Folder, you will have a folder 100MYFOL and the image files in it will start at PS10001.

Copyright Information

You can set the **Artist** name and **Copyright Holder** and record them in each picture's **EXIF** (Exchangeable image file format) file. In today's free for all Internet it doesn't count for much but it's worth covering yourself for the sake of it. **Display Copyright Info.** lets you confirm what you have entered.

Setup Menu - Monitor / Display 1

Power Save Mode

Sleep Mode

Set this to the minimum that doesn't annoy you. Note that if you are using a **Custom** setting and have altered it, when you wake the camera up by half pressing the shutter release it will have reverted to the **Custom** setting. So, if you are using a **Custom** setting that is set to **4:3 Aspect Ratio** but you have altered it to **16:9** in the **Aspect Ratio** menu, if the camera goes into **Sleep** mode, when you wake it, it will have reverted to **4:3**.

Sleep Mode(Wi-Fi)

set to **On** If the Wi-Fi is active but not connected to anything for 15 minutes, it will automatically turn off. Wi-Fi is a heavy drain on the camera battery so this is a useful precaution.

Auto LVF/Monitor Off

Again, set this to the minimum that doesn't annoy you. The EVF and monitor are big consumers of battery energy so the shorter this setting the better. Touch any button or the monitor to resume normal viewing. This does not reset the **Custom** setting. Using the previous example, if it went off in **16:9**, it will resume in **16:9**

Power Save LVF Shooting

This is an extreme but not too inconvenient power saving ploy. It can put the camera to sleep after as little as 1 second of inactivity. The camera wakes up quickly with a half push on the shutter button so it is not too onerous for the battery saving potential. You can have it operate only while **Control Panel** is displayed or **While Recording Standby**, meaning ant time you leave the camera idle. This has the potential to double the number of shots per battery charge. It drives some people mad, however! Note that if you are using **C**ustom mode and have altered the setting, it will revert to the recorded **C** mode. So, if you are using **Custom 1** which is recorded as Aperture Priority mode, f/4, ISO200 and change the settings to Shutter priory, f/16, ISO1600, when the camera is woken up from **Power Save LVF Shooting** it will be back at Aperture Priority, f/4, ISO200. Loading a setting from **Save/Restore Camera Settings** will avoid that so that the S1 will come back with the settings with which it turned off.

Monitor Frame Rate

60fps gives smoother viewing, use **30**fps to reduce battery consumption a little. I opt for the smoother viewing.

LVF Frame Rate

120fps or **60**fps. I prefer the smoother viewing of 120fps,even if it does use a bit more battery power.

Monitor Settings

This can adjust **Brightness**, **Contrast**, **Saturation**, **Red Tint** and **Blue Tint** of the monitor and viewfinder.**Note:** There is wizardry afoot here! If you view the menu through the **EVF**, you will see **Viewfinder**. If you view the menu on the monitor, you will see **Monitor Display**. The alterations you make will be stored and applied to the EVF or Monitor separately. I find the default neutral settings to my taste and leave this alone.

Monitor Backlight

sets the brightness of the monitor and/or EVF. Set to **Auto**, brightness is adjusted automatically. I find Auto brightness works best for me.

Remaining Battery Level

You can have the battery level displayed as a bar or as a percentage.

Status-LCD

You can disable its illumination altogether or set it **High** or **Low**. You can also choose to have it show battery level, the card in use and the number of shots left when the camera is off. The battery overhead for this is tiny.

Eye Sensor

Sensitivity

When **LVF/ Monitor Switch** is set to auto, this controls how easily it switches between monitor and EVF. Experience will tell you which is best for you but I find **LOW** minimizes unwanted switching when using the monitor and your sleeve goes near the EVF mounted sensor. It can be very irritating!

LVF/Monitor Switch

The S1 will switch automatically between EVF and Monitor as move your eye to and from the EVF. However, when you have the camera on a tripod and the **Sensitivity** set to **Low** your arm or hand can come close enough to the switching sensor to make it switch when you don't want it to. This item enables you to explicitly set the viewing to EVF or Monitor. There's the **LVF** button on the EVF housing which is a better way of setting this, since it steps through Auto/EVF/Monitor directly.

Setup Menu - Monitor / Display 2

Level Gauge Adjust.

The **Level Gauge** comes preset. If you find it inaccurate, put the camera on a known level surface or set it level with one of the accessory spirit levels that fits in the flash hot shoe. Press **Adjust** and that will be your new **Level**.

Setup Menu - IN/OUT

Beep

From here you can control the main beep volume, the AF confirmation beep volume and tone and the volume and tone of the electronic shutter. I do like having my S1 sound like an old Rolleiflex!

Headphone Volume

When you plug headphones in to the S1 to monitor video sound you can vary the volume here. Rotating the **Control Dial** will do the same thing.

Wi-Fi

Note: The Wi-Fi connections are too dependent on the devices being connected to for detailed instructions to be very useful. The best way is to follow the camera's on screen instructions. If, after entering the password for your Wi-Fi network, you see Manual, you are expected to input the name of the device. If you aren't sure, take a look at your router's connections page where it will list all the devices connected to it. If you want to connect to your PC, put in its name listed in the router. If you want to send pictures to your PC or other device, it must have a folder(s) set up as a **Share**. so, if you want to connect to your PC, called MYPC, after you enter that, you will see a list of your **Share**d folders to select from. For connections to a phone, I just start up Wi-Fi on the camera and then look for its SSID, S1-###### in the list of available Wi-Fi connections, then start the **Lumix Sync**

New Connection
• **Remote Shooting & View** - for connecting to your smartphone
• **Send Images While Recording** - you can send pictures as you take them to your smartphone, PC, laptop, or via **web service** to Google Drive etc. You can also send them for temporary storage via the **Lumix Club.** They are copied to the destination and remain available on your card(s)
• **Send Images Stored in the Camera** - as above but you select the images to send after taking. You can send them directly to a printer as well as the options above

Select a destination from History
  this stores previous connections so that you can go straight to them without the setup procedure very time. If you press the **Register to Favorite** box at the bottom of the screen, the connection will be stored in the Favorites.

Select a destination from Favorite
  Your chosen most used connections stored for easy access.

Wi-Fi Setup
Priority of Remote device
• **Camera** - when connected to your phone you can change settings via your phone or as normal on the S1. The limitation is that camera dial settings cannot be changed on the phone
• **Smartphone** - settings can only be made on the phone but you can change the dial settings
Wi-Fi Password

If you are seriously concerned about someone stealing your images while transferring them via **Wi-Fi** you should make sure this is set **On** before making a connection.

Lumix Club

You can set up, delete or add a **Lumix Club** account here. You can transfer images to social media sites and other web services via **Lumix Club**. Touch **Set Login ID** and you will be given a **Login ID** number. Touch **Password** to set a password of your choice. Now go the **Lumix Club** web site and enter these. You will be presented with several options, among them to transfer images directly to Google Drive etc.

Workgroup

By default on Windows this is WORKGROUP. If you go to Control Panel in Windows - you will find the Workgroup name there. If it is different, set it here.

Device Name

When you see your S1 listed in the available Wi-Fi networks on your smartphone or tablet it will be S1 followed by a series of numbers. You can set any name you like here and that will be the one you see listed. Technically this is the camera's SSID.

Wi-Fi Function Lock

enables you to set a password that must be entered before Wi-Fi will start at all.

Network Address

For information only. Displays the Media Access Control (MAC) address of the camera. This is a unique hardware identifier for the device. The IP address is assigned by the device to which it is connected.

Bluetooth

The connecting procedure the first time will depend on your device but essentially you need to go to **Set→Pairing** which will put the S1 in **Pairing** mode bring up a screen with the S1's device name (also known as the SSID). Open up the **Lumix Sync** app and a message about camera registration comes up. Follow the instructions. If you don't see that message, touch the ? icon top left of the Lumix Sync home page and hit **Camera Registration (pairing)** an follow the instructions. Once you have paired your phone and the S1, it should connect automatically next time. You can use the Bluetooth connection as a remote release via the Lumix Sync app but if you want to control the camera as well you will need the Wi-Fi connection which can be initiated from the app. **Note:** images sent to your phone will be found in an Album called **LumixSync**.

• **Send Image (smartphone)** - the easiest way to do this is to press import images on the Sync app. This will connect you to the Camera's Wi-Fi and display the images stored in the camera. Pres **Select** and you can choose the images to send by touching them. A press on the **Send** icon at the bottom of the page will send the pictures to wherever you have set the default picture storage on your smartphone, the same place pictures taken with your phone are stored. It's obviously best to have an SD card with plenty of capacity inserted in your phone, given the size of the S1'a image files

• **Remote Wakeup** - with this enabled, you can turn the camera on from the Sync app, even if the power switch is off. Handy if the camera is set up somewhere inaccessible

• **Returning from Sleep Mode** - if you have **Remote Wakeup** set **On** can shorten the time the camera takes to wake up and sort itself out. Set to **Remote Shutter Priority**, the camera treats the smartphone as a remote shutter release which only needs a Bluetooth connection. Set to **Remote/Transfer Priority** it must fire up the Wi-Fi connection too, so is slower

• **Auto Transfer** - this sets the S1 to send images to your smartphone as they are taken. This works pretty well since you can keep taking pictures while the images are transferred. You'll need a good sized SD card in the phone!

• **Location Logging** - very useful for travel photography. Set **On**, **GPS** information will be written to your images as they are taken. The location data is sent from your phone to the S1 so this relies on your phone's GPS Location data being switched on and being in a location where GPS can operate. When this is in operation, an icon appears on screen. If it flashes, your phone does not have a GPS signal

• **Auto Clock Set** - Since your smartphone will be getting accurate time signals from the Internet, this will keep the camera time up to date and synced with your smartphone

• **Wi-Fi Network Settings** - This enables you to connect conveniently to a Wi-Fi network without leaving the **Bluetooth** menu

USB

Sets how the USB3 slot will will be used.

• **Select on connection** - This asks you which connection you want when you plug the cable in
• **PC(Storage)** - this treats the camera as a storage device so the slots will appear as dives **D:** and **E:** for example
• **PC(Tether)** - this allows the S1 to be operated by the **Lumix Tether** program running on any Windows or Mac machine
• **Pictbridge(PTP)** - Set to this if you want to connect to a **Pictbridge** printer to print directly from the camera

USB Power Supply

Set **On**, the battery will be charged via by the USB cable even when shooting. If you use the supplied AC Adapter, the camera charges whether this setting is on or off.

Battery Information

This tells you the level of charge remaining in the battery. This information is readily available on the **Status LCD** of course. More interesting is the Battery Health indicator. All batteries lose their ability to hold a charge over the course of time and the number of pictures you can take on a charge diminishes. You can see how far this process has progressed graphically here. Thankfully, with modern high quality batteries this deterioration is quite slow. Information is also given on the state of the grip battery, if fitted.

Battery Use Priority

If you have Panasonic's accessory battery grip fitted, this determines which battery is used first. It is probably more convenient to use the grip battery first and treat the body battery as a backup, since if the body battery is used first you have to remove the grip to change it.

TV Connection

HDMI Mode (Playback)

When connecting to your TV with the HDMI cable, sets the output resolution compatible with your TV. You may need to look at the manual for your TV if you have a problem with this. Normally, set this to **Auto** and the TV will tell the S1 its output resolution without your intervention

HLG View Assist (HDMI)

If you are outputting to an external monitor via HDMI this sets how the images will look. If you set this item to **Mode1** or **mode2**, images will be viewed and displayed in a natural looking form.
Mode1converts with an emphasis on the reproduction of bright areas like the sky. **Mode2** emphasizes the reproduction for the main subject and will be the generally more useful one. **Auto** makes the choice for you according to the external monitor's capability.

Viera Link

If you have a **Viera** compatible TV and connect the camera to it with an **HDMI** cable, you can control the camera with the TV's remote control.

Setup Menu - Setting

Save to Custom Mode

Custom Modes are one of the most useful facilities on digital cameras. They store a set of settings for instant recall at a turn of the **Mode Dial**. Let's say you set up the S1 with the basic working settings I offer in the **My Examples** section of this book. They work fine but you are photographing some sports so want to use a higher shutter speed and ISO, JPG instead of RAW+JPG and Focus Peaking. No problem. But when you switch the S1 off and then on again next day, it loads with the last settings used. Do your remember what you altered? To get it back to **My Example** you are going to have to look at the book and set it all back to how it was. A pain! Except that you have **Custom Mode**s. Set the S1 up according to **My Example**. Set that to **Custom Mode C1**. Confirm the Overwrite current Camera settings dialog. Those settings are now registered to **C1**. If you leave the camera on **C1**, no matter how you alter those settings, when you switch the camera off and then on, it will always open with that array of settings. If you switch away from **C1** to **iA**, for example, and then switch back, again you will have the **My Example** settings. I see the **Custom Mode**(s)as a way of taming and managing the complexities of a digital camera. You have 3 **Custom Mode**s available on the **Mode Dial** for instant recall of arrays of settings but **C3** itself can store up to 10 arrays of settings in the form of **C3-1**, **C3-2** etc. When you set the **Mode Dial** to **C3** you can select which flavour of **C3 C3-1**, **C3-2** etc by pressing **Menu/SetNote:** a more memorable name can be given to **Custom Mode**s if you press the **Disp.** when the **Overwrite** dialog appears.

Load Custom Mode

Select a **Custom Mode** and load it to your current **Mode Dial** setting. This really needs to be invoked according to the **Mode Dial** setting it was in when saved. If your **Custom Mode C1** includes settings of Aperture Priority, 51200**ISO** and you load with the **Mode Dial** set to **S**hutter priority, it can't change the **Mode Dial** setting to **A**, which will remain in **P** but it will set the **ISO** to 51200.

Custom Mode Settings

Limit No. of Custom Mode

As mentioned earlier, **Custom Mode C3** can register up to 10 settings in the form **C3-1**→**C3-10** (These identifiers can be changed to more memorable names). To see a long list when you want to invoke a new **C3** setting can be tedious so this enables to to limit how many **C3** settings you can set. For many photographers the three **Custom Modes** on the **Mode Dial** will be enough so this can be set to one to avoid any confusion.

Edit Title

The cryptic **C1**, **C3-2** designations are not user friendly so you can change them to something more memorable here. The name can be up to twenty two characters long so there's plenty of room for something descriptive.

How to Reload Custom Mode

While use a **Custom Mode**, you are likely to want to change some settings temporarily from the saved ones. This setting determines when the settings will be returned to the saved ones and your temporary changes discarded.

• **Change Recording Mode** - With this **On**, if you are using **C1** but have changed the **ISO**, if you switch to Shutter Priority and then back again, your **ISO** value will have changed back to the saved one. Set **Off** it would have retained your change

• **Return From Sleep Mode** - Set **On**, if your camera goes into **Sleep** mode any temporary change to **C1** would be lost when the camera was woken up. Set **Off** and any change made would still be in force. One of my main gripes against the **Custom Modes** in the past has been the loss of any temporary change made when the camera goes to sleep. If you were shooting with **Power Save LVF Shooting** set to 5 seconds and had temporarily switched on **Peaking** you'd need to turn **Peaking** on over and over again. This setting avoids that

• **Turn the Power ON** - set to **Off**, when you turn the camera off, any temporary changes are retained when power is switched on again. This rather defeats the use of **Custom Modes** for me since I will almost certainly have forgotten what changes I had made. Set **On** you always open the camera with a known raft of settings

Select Loading Details

When you use **Load Custom Mode**, this determines whether the **F** stop/Shutter Speed, **ISO** and **White Balance** are set along with all the other settings. With all these set **On** if you are shooting in Aperture mode and using a settings of f/8, **ISO** 6400 and **White Balance/ Sunshine** and then load a **Custom Mode** which has settings of f/4, **ISO**200, **AWB**, your present settings f/8 etc will be retained while all the other **Custom** settings like **Peaking**, **Aspect Ratio** are loaded. With these settings **Off** the **Custom** Settings will be loaded and override your present settings.

Save/Restore Camera Setting

This allows you to save whatever settings you are using currently to a named file stored on a card in either of the card slots. That file and any others you save (up to 10 are allowed) will be saved in a folder called **CAMSET**. That folder can then be copied over to external storage and in the event of a card failure, loss or format, copied over to a new card. When you have put a lot of work in to a set of **Custom Mode**s it is reassuring to back them up and know that they can be reinstalled any time you wish. A good strategy is

• Set the S1 up for a given task, say Cycling

• Save that set up to **C1** and rename it to Cycle

• Do the same for any other setups you wish and save those as C2/ C3-1/ C3-2 and so on renamed to their task as with Cycle

• Set the **Mode Dial** the **Custom** setting Cycle and **Save** it as, say, C1Cycle

• Copy the **CAMSET** folder to your PC and you now have a backup for all your **Custom** settings

• In future, if you amend any settings and want to keep them, say you want Cycle to operate with the **ELEC.** rather than the **MECH.**shutter previously set, just overwrite Cycle with the new setting and copy the whole **CAMSET** folder over to your PC

• If you rename the first **CAMSET** folder **CAMSET_OLD** you can keep both versions. If you

want to reload the original settings, just rename
CAMSET to **CAMSET_2**, say, and rename
CAMSETOLD to **CAMSET** and copy it back over to
the card

Note: if you are lucky enough to have two S1s or a
friend or colleague has one, you can share all your
Saved settings just by copying them over to one of
the cards on the new S1. You can, if you wish have
both **Custom** settings and **Saved** settings but 20
setting sets get very unwieldy. One big difference
between **Custom** and **Saved** settings is that if you
change any of the settings after **Loading** them, if
you switch the camera on and off, the changed
settings will still be there.

Reset

This allows you to selectively **Reset** aspects of the
camera settings. **Rec.** will bring all the Recording
settings - basically the **Photo** and **Video** back to their
defaults. **Network settings** deletes all your
Bluetooth and **Wi-Fi** connections and settings only.
The last dialog will reset **Setup** menu and **Custom**
but leave your **Wi-Fi**, **Bluetooth** and **Photo/ Video**
settings in place.

Setup Menu - Others

Clock Set

Self explanatory.

Style

You have the usual choice of display modes, 12/24hr and European or American date standards.

Time Zone

Set the S1 to your time zone.

Pixel Refresh

I've never come across them myself since I've been digital cameras but it is possible that sensor pixels become ineffective and give bright pin pricks of random coloured pixels in your images. **Pixel Refresh** will identify and correct them. It probably does this by comparing them with surrounding pixels and picking a similar tone for the inaccurate one(s). It doesn't sound ideal what's a few pixels among 24,000,000?

Sensor Cleaning

The sensor is cleaned every time you turn the camera on by a magnetic mechanism shaking the sensor at very high speed. It simply has the effect of dislodging dust. If you see dust on the sensor when changing lenses or in the form of 'dust bunnies' on your images, you can run the **Sensor Cleaning** any time (and as often) as you wish. **Note:** Any dust present is not on the sensor itself but on a protective clear filter in front of it. When you see a dark patch on an image, usually on an even toned part such as a clear blue sky what you are seeing is not the dust but its shadow falling on the sensor. Mostly the camera's

66

Sensor Cleaning dislodges it but if it does not, you may need to get it professionally cleaned. You can buy very good cleaning kits of you want to do it yourself but you will need to take care not to scratch the filter. Having said that, the filter is tough and soft lint free cloth will never scratch it. How do you get lint free cloth? A thin cotton T-shirt cut up into cloths and washed many times will be lint free. Most dust on a sensor will never be seen since the lenses are usually used at f/4 or so. That means that when the light arrives at the sensor the shadow of the dust is diffused. If you want to see check for any dust, stop the lens down to f/22 and look at an even toned area of your image. I personally don't go looking for it since I usually shoot at f/4 or wider and it is not a problem. **Note:** Precautions against gathering dust are: make sure the rear of the lens is clean before fitting it. When you do change lenses, try to hold the camera mouth downwards. The worst stuff to get on the sensor is pollen. It can stick and be impervious to the vibration cleaning of the camera. If it does stick some kind of wet cleaning will be necessary. You can buy suitable fluids as part of a cleaning kit.

Language

Comme vous voulez.

Firmware Version

Body Firmware and **Lens Firmware** versions are displayed. If you visit Panasonic web site, you will be able to see if there is a more recent version of the firmware available. You should keep firmware up to date to get the best from your equipment.

Firmware Update

When you have downloaded an update, install it here. The procedure worries many photographers but it is very straightforward and risk free. Make sure the battery is full as power loss during the update can be serious. The camera won't proceed if the power is too low.

• 1 Download the firmware from Panasonic's support site for your country

• 2 Extract the firmware update from the ZIP file you have downloaded to the root directory of an empty SD card. The file will have a name like S1V11.bin. On your file explorer, it should show as something like E:/ S1V11.bin. The E:/ is an example, it could be anything from E:/ to Z:/ according to how your computer allocates cards

• 3 Insert the card into the S1's slot with the camera **Off**

• 4 Switch on the power and press **Firmware Update**

• 5 Press **Menu/Set** and select **Yes**

• 6 Leave the camera to get on with it - it will notify you when the camera is ready for use again. It's usually a few minutes

• 7 When its done and the camera restarted, **Format** the card to get rid of the .bin file and carry on as usual

  Note: this is Panasonic's present procedure but it is as well to check it on their site when doing an upgrade.

Software info

  I have no idea why this is here.

Online Manual

  This gives you information on how to access the online manual. The manual itself doesn't appear on the camera, unfortunately.

Playback Menu - Mode

Rotate Disp.

With this **Off**, a picture shot in portrait orientation when reviewed on the monitor will be played back in portrait orientation, meaning you must turn the camera to see it properly. With this **On**, the portrait orientated pictures are displayed rotated to landscape orientation. It is more convenient but means the image will have a black band either side and occupy only a portion of the monitor.

Picture Sort

Plays back images in the order they were taken or by filename. A lot of the time this will amount to the same thing, of course.

Magnify From AF Point

A clever one, this. If we assume that the part of the scene we chose to focus on is the area that we most require to be sharp this enables us to check that part immediately. Set **On**, when you turn the rear dial to magnify the image, wherever the camera focused at the time of taking is the area which is enlarged.

LUT View Assist (Monitor)

If you have applied an LUT in **Setup→Monitor / Display 3V-Log View Assist** you can quickly activate or de-activate it here for reviewing of video on the monitor.

HLG View Assist (Monitor)

Improves the viewing of **HLG** images. With this **Off** the images appear flat and lifeless. **Mode1** and **Mode2** improve the appearance of sky and bright areas or the main subject respectively. The image itself is not affected, only how it displays.

Playback Menu - Process Image

RAW Processing

If you shoot **RAW** images you can process and covert them to **JPG** here. I can't think of a better way to illustrate the efficacy of the **RAW** than this. You can alter almost any characteristic of the image from **Photo Style** to the **Noise Reduction** via **Saturation** and **White Balance**. Having done the processing you wish, press **RAW→JPG** and you are shown the original image ad your version side by side. If you like what you see, press **Yes** and it is done. Under **More Settings** on the carousel, you can change the **Picture Size** the image, assign it a **Color Space**. **Note:** if you have recorded an **HLG** you can choose to have its display enhanced on the camera monitor or an external **HDMI** one if that is what you are using. If all else fails, hit **Revert To Original** and all your lovingly done edits will be discarded.

6L/4K PHOTO Bulk Saving

When you have shot a 6K/4K burst it is in the form of an **mp4** video file. If you want to examine a sequence of the files in detail this facility will output up to 5 seconds of the sequence in the form of separate **JPG** files If your sequence is longer than 5 seconds, you can choose the the start point and files will be output from there. If it is less, all the files will be extracted.

• When you open this menu item, the **6K/4K** files only are displayed. Scroll though and select the one you want to **Bulk Save**

• Press **Set** and then **Yes** in the following dialog box
• The **Bulk Saving** will take a few seconds to a minute or so depending on how many files are to be processed
• If the **Playback** screen shows only one file, turn the rear dial one click left to bring up the **Thumbnail**s
• You can identify your **Bulk Save**(s) by the **Group icon (Fig 63)**
• Touch that thumbnail and you can scroll through all the extracted frames with the Cursors or Joystick . The filename and position in the sequence/number in the sequence are displayed top left

Note: if you are shooting a 30fps sequence, a 5 second chunk will give you 150 files of around 4MB each so the space requirements should be kept in mind. Although you can only access the individual files by scrolling through the **Group** on the S1's monitor, if you connect the S1 to your PC or plug the card in to a reader, you will see all the extracted images separately in your file browser.

6K/4K PHOTO Noise Reduction

When you extract and save an image from a **6K/4K** sequence this will apply noise reduction to it if the **ISO** is high. You can either switch the **NR** off altogether or leave it to the camera. That doesn't stop you from denoising the image for yourself in post processing, of course.**Note:** this does not work with **Bulk Saved** images.

Time Lapse Video

If you don't create a video from a **Time Lapse** sequence at the time you make it, you can create it here or create another sequence with different parameters. The sequences are identified by the same

Group icon used in **Bulk Saving**. You have a great range of options here.

• **OK** - means make the **Time Lapse Video** with the settings below

• **Rec Quality** - Everything from **4K** to **FHD** here

• **Frame Rate** - the faster the **Frame Rate** the smoother the video. 50fps is probably a bit OTT for most purposes, 15 the the minimum for a smooth(ish) result

• **Sequence** - you can have the video play for from first to last frame shot or backwards. This is more useful in **Stop Motion Video** where it is easier to shoot something frame by frame going from an organized state to a chaotic one and then show it backwards to give the impression of time going the wrong way

Stop Motion Video

The same as Time Lapse Video

Playback Menu - Edit Info

Protect

You can protect images from deletion by selecting
and **Set**ting them. You will see a **Key** icon on
protected images. **Note:** This only protects images
from the **Delete** function. If you **Format** a card, it
will clear all the images on the card, protected or not.

Rating

You can assign a **Rating** from 1 to 5 stars for
images. Just press **Set** to bring them up on screen.
One assigned the ratings can be viewed in the Details
section of the file's properties in Windows but
Lightroom doesn't appear to see them. **Note:** if you
are Deleting files and some have ratings, you are
given the opportunity to either **Delete All** or **Delete
All Non-Rating**.

Playback Menu - Edit Image

Resize

You can reduce the size of up to 100 images in one swoop with this. The options are **M**edium and **S**mall and you are given a list of what the sizes will be in whichever **Aspect Ratio** the original is in. You can either **Resize** the original image or **Save as New Picture**, probably the safer option. A handy facility if you know your picture will be for a web page or email attachment.**Note:** you can't **Resize**, **HLG** or **High Resolution** images.

Rotate

You can **Rotate** an image in 90° steps.

Video Divide

Select a **Video** or **6K/4K** burst file and split it in two. After you have selected your file, you will see the usual video playback controls. Play the Video and pause it at the point you want to cut it. You will see a scissors icon. Touch that and the video will be divided at that point.

Copy

This allows you to **Copy** files from one card slot to the other. All you need to do is select the file(s) or a folder to **Copy** or **Copy All in Folder**. They will be copied to a new folder on the other card. **Note: Protected** files will lose their **Protection** when copied and need to have it reset.

Playback Menu - Others

Delete Confirmation

When you are Deleting an image, the confirmation screen by default highlights the **No** option. You can save a key press here by setting this to **"Yes" first**

<u>My Example Menu</u>

Photo Menu

- **Photo Style - STD**
- **Metering Mode** - Multi-metering (top icon)
- **Aspect Ratio - 3:2**
- **Picture Quality** - RAW+FINE or JPG only if preferred
- **Picture Size - L 24m**
- **HLG Photo - OFF**
- **High Resolution Mode - OFF**
- **Long Exposure NR - ON**

Photo Menu - Image Quality 2

- **ISO Sensitivity (photo) - 100/6400**
- **Min shutter Speed - 1/30**
- **i.Dynamic Range - OFF**
- **Vignetting Comp - OFF**
- **Diffraction Compensation - OFF/ ON for movie**
- **Filter Settings - OFF**

Photo Menu - Focus

- **AF Custom Setting(Photo) - Set 1**
- **AF Assist Light - ON**
- **Focus Peaking - ON**
- **1-Area AF Moving Speed - FAST**

Photo Menu - Flash 1

- **Flash Mode** - Forced Flash On
- **Firing Mode - TTL**
- **Flash Adjust - 0**
- **Flash Synchro - 1st**
- **Manual Flash Adjust** - Depends on flash
- **Auto Exposure Comp - off**

- **Red-Eye Removal - off**
- **Wireless** - off

Photo Menu - Flash 2

- **Wireless Channel - N/A**
- **Wireless FP - N/A**
- **Communication Light - N/A**
- **Wireless Setup - N/A**

Photo Menu - Others (Photo)1

- **Bracketing** - OFF (3. 1 when used 0/-/+/; Burst Setting)
- **Silent Mode - OFF**
- **Image Stabilizer** - Normal HALF-SHUTTER OFF OFF
- **Burst Shot 1 Setting** - H (MECH. shutter and using AFC)
- **Burst Shot 2 Setting - 6K**
- **Shutter Type** - ELEC. (MECH. for flash and long exposures)
- **Shutter Delay - OFF**
- **Ex. Tele Conv. - OFF**

Photo Menu - Others (Photo) 2

- **Time Lapse/ Animation - N?A**
- **Self Timer - N/A**
- **Flicker Decrease (Photo) - OFF**
- **6K/4K PHOTO** - 6K Pre-Burst
- **Post Focus - OFF**
- **Multiple Exposure - N/A**

Video Menu - Image Quality 1

- **Exposure Mode - S** and set shutter speed to 2x frame rate
- **Photo Style - STD**

- **Metering Mode** - Multi-Metering
- **ISO Sensitivity(video) - 100 AUTO**
- **Flicker Decrease(Video) - OFF**
- **i.Dynamic Range - OFF**
- **Vignetting Comp. - OFF**
- **Diffraction Compensation - OFF**

Video Menu - Image Quality 1

- **Filter Settings - OFF**
- **Auto Exposure in P/A/S/M - ON**
- **Creative Video Combined Set** - All set to camera (stills) icon

Video Menu - Image Format

- **Rec Quality** - To choice -for YouTube I use FHD 20M 30p
- **High Speed Video - N?A**
- **Rec File Format - MP4**
- **Luminance Level - 16-255**

Video Menu - Focus

- **AF Custom Setting(Video) - 0 0**
- **Continuous AF - ON**
- **Focus Peaking - ON**
- **1-Area AF Moving Speed - FAST**

Video Menu - Audio

- **Sound Rec Level Display - ON**
- **Sound Rec Level Adjust - AS needed**
- **Sound Rec Level Limiter - ON**
- **Wind Noise Canceller** - STANDARD (OFF if indoors)
- **Mic Socket** - As applicable
- **Special Mic - N?A**
- **XLR Mic Adapter Setting - N/A**

• **Sound Output** - REALTIME
Video Menu - Monitor / Display

• **HDMI Rec Output - N/A**
Video Menu - Others(Video)

• **Image Stabilizer** - Normal (top icon) HALF SHUTTER OFF OFF
• **Image Area of Video - FULL**
Custom Menu - Image Quality

• **Photo Style Settings - To Choice**
• **ISO Increments - 1EV**
• **Extended ISO - OFF**
• **Exposure Offset Adjust. - All 0**
• **Color Space - sRGB**
• **Exposure Comp Reset - ON**
Custom Menu - Focus Shutter 1

• **Focus/Shutter Priority** - AFS FOCUS AFC BALANCE
• **Focus Switching for Vert / Hor - OFF**
• **AF/AE Lock Hold - OFF**
• **AF+MF** - OFF
• **MF Assist** - ON OFF OFF PIP
• **MF Guide - ON**
• **Focus Ring Lock - OFF**
• **Show/Hide MF Mode - To choice**
Custom Menu - Focus Shutter 2

• **Pinpoint AF Setting - MID PIP**
• **AF-Point Scope Setting - OFF PIP**
• **Shutter AF - ON**
• **Half-Press Shutter - OFF**
• **Quick AF - OFF**

- **Eye Sensor AF - ON**
- **Looped Focus Frame - OFF**
- **AFC Start Point (225 Area) - OFF**

Custom Menu - Operation 1

- **Q.Menu Settings** - MODE 1 Value
- **Touch Settings** - ON OFF AF OFF
- **Lock Lever Setting** - Touch Screen locked/ all others Unlocked
- **Fn Button Set** - To Choice
- **Fn Lever Setting** - Shutter Type MODE 2 Setting ELEC.
- **WB/ISO/Expo. Button - WHILE PRESSING**
- **ISO Displayed Setting - ISO/ISO**
- **Exposure Comp. Disp. Setting** - OFF COMP/COMP (top icons)

Custom Menu - Operation 2

- **Dial Set** - SET 2 (Control Dial Assignment Headphone) (Exposure Comp. OFF)
- **Joystick Setting - D.Focus**
- **Illuminated Button - ON 2**
- **Video Rec Button (Remote) - ON**

Custom Menu - Monitor / Display 1

- **Auto Review** - OFF HOLD HOLD ON
- **Constant Preview - ON**
- **Level Gauge - OFF**
- **Histogram** - OFF
- **Photo Grid Line - OFF**
- **Framing Outline - OFF**
- **Center Marker - OFF**
- **AF Area Display - ON**

Custom Menu - Monitor / Display 2

- **Live View Boost - OFF**
- **Monochrome Live View - OFF**
- **Night Mode - OFF**
- **LVF/Monitor Disp. Set** - Icons Outside Icons Inside
- **Expo.Meter** - OFF
- **Focal Length - N/A**
- **Photo/Video Preview - Still camera**
- **Photos/Videos Remaining - Photos**

Custom Menu - Monitor / Display 3

- **Show/Hide Monitor Layout - Both ON**
- **Blinking Highlights - OFF**
- **Zebra Pattern - ON**
- **HLG View Assist - OFF**
- **Sheer Overlay - OFF**
- **I.S. Status Scope - OFF**

Custom Menu - Lens / Others

- **Lens Focus Resume - OFF**
- **Focus Ring Control** - NON-LINEAR 300°

Setup Menu - Card/File

- **Card Format - N/A**
- **Double Card Slot Function** - ALLOCATION REC RAW 6K/4K Video→2 (JPG→1)
- **Folder / File Settings - Defaults**
- **File Number Reset - N/A**
- **Copyright Information - ON ON**

Setup Menu - Monitor / Display 1

- **Power Save Mode** - 5MIN ON 5MIN Power Save LVF Shooting 5SEC CONTROL PANEL (if maxing battery life)
- **Monitor Frame Rate - 60fps**
- **LVF Frame Rate - 120fps**

- **Monitor Settings** - ALL 0 (Defaults)
- **Monitor Backlight - AUTO**
- **Remaining Battery Level - %**
- **Status-LCD** - H ON
- **Eye Sensor** - LOW LVF/MON AUTO

Setup Menu - Monitor / Display 2

- **Level Gauge Adjust. - N/A**

Setup Menu - IN/OUT

- **Beep** - All VOL Mid Both Tone 1
- **Headphone Volume - 3**
- **Wi-Fi** - N/A
- **Bluetooth** - N/A
- **USB** - Select On connection ON
- **Battery Information - N/A**
- **Battery Use Priority - N/A**
- **TV Connection - As TV**

Setup Menu - Setting

- **Save to Custom Mode - N/A**
- **Load Custom Mode - N/A**
- **Custom Mode Settings - N/A**
- **Save/Restore Camera Setting - N/A**
- **Reset** - N/A

Setup Menu - Others

- **Clock Set - N/A**
- **Time Zone - N/A**
- **Pixel Refresh - N/A**
- **Sensor Cleaning - N/A**
- **Language** - N/A
- **Firmware Version - N/A**
- **Online Manual - N/A**

Playback Menu - Mode

- **Rotate Disp. - ON**
- **Picture Sort** - DATE/TIME
- **Magnify From AF Point - OFF**
- **HLG View Assist (Monitor - MODE 2**

Playback Menu - Process Image

- -
- **RAW Processing - N/A**
- **6L/4K PHOTO Bulk Saving -**
- **6K/4K PHOTO Noise Reduction - OFF**
- **Time Lapse Video - N/A**
- **Stop Motion Video -N/A**

Playback Menu - Edit Info

- **Protect** - N/A
- **Rating** - N/A

Playback Menu - Edit Image

- **Resize** - N/A
- **Rotate** - N/A
- **Video Divide - N/A**
- **Copy -**

Playback Menu - Others

- **Delete Confirmation - "Yes" first**

Addendum

Here are few items of information that didn't fit logically into the rest of the book. They are in no articular order and some are intended for first time users of mirrorless cameras.

Cleaning the camera

Viewfinder

The eye cup has a small catch right at the bottom, underneath the eyecup. Press the catch in to the body and rotate the eye cup a quarter turn or so anti-clockwise. Blow the dirt away and then give a light wipe over with a lens cleaning cloth.

Sensor

The camera give the sensor a hypersonic shake every time it starts up and that dislodges most of the dirt. It's probably wise to keep your cleaning to a blow with a 'rocket' style blower. Just make sure the blower doesn't go beyond the lens mount as any touch of the sensor carries a risk of scratching. Having said that, you can't scratch the sensor itself since it it is behind a protective glass cover. I'm happy enough to use commercially available cleaning swabs such these - https://amzn.to/2ITRal7 but I'd stress that you need a certain amount of confidence to do it and if you are unsure, give it to a professional. You'll know you have dirt on the sensor when you see blemishes on evenly lit single coloured image areas such as the sky or a blank, light coloured wall. That blemish or spot is not actually the dirt itself but its shadow from the glass sensor protector. you'll only see it when the camera is well stopped down, beyond about f/11. At apertures wider than that, the shadow is so diffuse that it can't be seen and, you could argue, doesn't matter. To check for dirt on the sensor, stop the lens down to f/22 and point the camera at a plain white surface. A sheet of A4 paper will do nicely. Fill the frame with the A4 sheet. The camera won't be able to focus on it but it doesn't matter. Now take a shot and examine it on your computer looking for those spots. **Note:** one of the worst things to get on a sensor is pollen. It is very sticky and difficult to remove without a wet cleaner and swab. Avoid dirt falling on the sensor by changing lenses while holding the mouth of the camera pointing to the ground. Mirrorless cameras will always be a little more susceptible to dirt on the sensor simply because there is no mirror to stop it.

Manual Exposure with ISOAuto

Some subjects by their nature require specified minimum exposure settings. A macro shot of a spider could be an example, where you might need a shutter speed of at least 1/125th to freeze any movement by the creature but also an aperture of f/11 to give enough depth of field. But what if the light is subject to change as you shoot? **A** or **S** will allow alterations to the speed or aperture you need. The answer is **M**anual mode which will maintain your settings. Then set the camera as you need and choose **ISOAuto**. The S1 will now raise and lower the **ISO** to maintain correct exposure. The downside is that if the light drops low you may have a more noisy image than you wished for but something has to give and the S1's large sensor should insure noise stays within acceptable bounds.

<u>Why Can't I Set ....?</u>

If some settings are unavailable, greyed out, make sure you are **not** set to shoot with

• **Post Focus**
• **Bracketing**
• **High Resolution**
• **HLG**
• **Burst Mode 1 or 2 on the Mode dial**
• **Can't shoot longer than 1 Second?** - check the shutter in use. Set it to **MECH.**, not **ELEC.** or **Silent**
• **Can't access XQD card?** - it won't work with the AVCHD video format